Leadership is
a art and a
science. This is
both. Enjoy!

Sandra

LEADING PEOPLE FROM THE MIDDLE

THE UNIVERSAL MISSION OF HEART AND MIND

WILLIAM P. ROBINSON

iUNIVERSE, INC.
NEW YORK   BLOOMINGTON

Leading People from the Middle
The Universal Mission of Heart and Mind

The views expressed in this work are solely those of the author and do not necessarily reflect the views of the publisher, and the publisher hereby disclaims any responsibility for them.

iUniverse books may be ordered through booksellers or by contacting:

iUniverse
1663 Liberty Drive
Bloomington, IN 47403
www.iuniverse.com
1-800-Authors (1-800-288-4677)

Because of the dynamic nature of the Internet, any Web addresses or links contained in this book may have changed since publication and may no longer be valid.

ISBN: 978-1-4401-8886-2 (sc)
ISBN: 978-1-4401-8889-3 (ebk)

Printed in the United States of America

iUniverse rev. date: 1/5/2010

Advance Praise for Leading People from the Middle

"Bill Robinson, an extraordinarily gifted leader of a flourishing university, offers vision and practical strategies for effective leadership. Moreover, he writes with wit and wisdom borne of his social-science expertise and street-smartened experience, making this a quick and captivating read. For leaders facing twenty-first century challenges, *Leading People from the Middle* offers hope and direction."

—David Myers, Social Psychologist, Hope College, author of seventeen books, including *Intuition: Its Powers and Perils*

"Simply writing about leadership is like finding guards for a basketball team; they are a dime a dozen. But when you find a guard that leads by word and action in all that he does, then you have found the diamond in the rough. Bill Robinson not only presents a great read, but he lives out the words in this book. I've witnessed first hand Bill's ability to lead within a community. As a former employee under Bill, I learned a great deal about leadership through watching and listening. The pages that follow are from a man that is talking the talk and walking the walk."

—Steve Alford, Head Coach, Men's Basketball, University of New Mexico

"Bill Robinson alerts us to the serious changes taking place in the leader's job and raises the crucial question of the relationship between organizations and society. Good stuff!"

—Max O. DePree, Former President/CEO of Herman Miller, Zeeland, Michigan

"*Leading People from the Middle is* a must read for today's managers who want to be tomorrow's business leaders. Dr. Robinson, a skillful author and educator, combines academic integrity with a warm personal style of writing to explain how the present-day style of management evolved and what it takes to become more effective in the current business environment."

—Charles L. Boppell, Former President and CEO, Worldwide Restaurant Concepts

"*Leading People from the Middle* accurately describes what happens on the Whitworth University campus under the leadership of Bill Robinson. It is very clear that Bill is called to be a leader. His is truly a leader from the middle—a consensus builder who is not afraid to make decisions. As you read his reflections, you have a very clear sense of him. He is genuine, generous, engaging, self-aware, and focused on the important issues and speaking the truth. When you're on Whitworth University campus, you see the wonderful camaraderie between Bill and the students. It is a very casual but mutually respectful relationship. Bill is genuinely interested in them and their experience. Yet, there is also no doubt about who the leader is. He is one of the best teachers and leaders through example these students could have—'leading from the middle.'"

—Violet A. Boyer, President/CEO, Independent Colleges of Washington

"Bill Robinson's vision of leadership comes from the right places— from his good heart, his deep belief in God, and his abiding faith in human nature. Those who share his vision will be free to be graceful and grateful leaders, prepared for the unexpected and excited for the opportunities that life and leadership present."

—George R. Nethercutt, Jr., Former Representative in Congress, Fifth District, Washington

"A 'must read' for executives in creative, fast-paced organizations. *Leading People from the Middle* does not imply weakness—just the opposite. In this extraordinarily thoughtful volume, Dr. William Robinson pieces together the best leadership lessons of the twentieth century with his sage views of the needs of the twenty-first century. He shows how vision, goals, direction, analysis, and 'opportunity seizing' can be combined with consensus building, decentralization, 'influencing from among,' and '*living* in the center of mission.' In so doing, he crafts a unique style of paradoxical leadership, which enables leaders to be 'laid back and aggressive, strong and vulnerable, caring and cold blooded,' depending upon the exigencies of situations and structures. Robinson has found a novel and implementable approach to leadership, which allows leaders to be at once optimally adaptable, open to opportunities, and above all, connected to organizational stakeholders."

—Robert J. Spitzer, Chancellor, Gonzaga University, Spokane, Washington

"In this book, one can see and watch Bill Robinson. For those who know him personally, we see lived each day the observations and lessons that Bill Robinson, the educator, has captured on these pages. What a joy it is to pick up a well-researched and written book and know that it is derived from a lived experience. A tireless individual, Bill draws energy from personal contact; so, in every way, the content of this book and any sequel that may follow is being written each and every day."

—Richard J. Umbdenstock, President/CEO, American Hospital Association, Chicago, Illinois

For Bonnie

CONTENTS

PREFACE

In the summer of 2000, I wrote *Leading People from the Middle*. It turned out pretty well. I tried to wrap good thinking from twentieth century leadership experts around my own findings and experiences. I still receive gratifying reports from folks who find the book quite helpful. That makes me feel great. I just reread the book myself. I think it remains worthwhile.

I'm not sure exactly what literary professionals mean by *voice*, but they all say it's the main thing in writing. When I ask them for a definition, I can't get a straight answer. Yet, they tell me they are deeply aware when this phantom is having its way with their pens. And they love it. Several folks have told me they could hear my voice in this book. I hope they consider that a compliment. My main goal for the book was to help folks become better leaders. I hope I accomplished that. And if the writing fairy was giving me *voice* tips while I was grinding out sentences, then props to her for helping me out.

So why am I rewriting this book? My original publisher wasn't very good at publishing. I got so frustrated that I bought the rights and inventory. I'm glad I did. Through Amazon.com and referrals, I've sold enough books from our garage to get our car back in there. In fact, I'm down to just a couple of boxes. So there are those two reasons. But even more, the world has changed and I've learned a lot since writing the book. I've spoken literally hundreds of times on leadership, and I've traded e-mails with many people who wrote me after reading the book. I've been enlightened from discussions with readers and people to whom I have spoken. My teachers have ranged from business executives to scholars to teachers.

I don't think I'd call this book a "second edition." Probably "a second try at the first edition" better describes it. This one is a little shorter, and of course that makes it a little better. I've carved off ideas that were met with shoulder shrugs, while expanding the ones that made the most sense to readers and listeners. For example, I heard from a pastor in western Washington who said the chapter on organizational structure caused him to completely reverse the way he thought of his ministry and his role. Others also found those ideas helpful. So, I fattened up that chapter.

Mainly, I rewrote this book because I felt I could make it better. And in a few years, I'm sure I'll feel the same way about the one in your hands.

Acknowledgments

For allowing me to work in their midst—the students, faculty, staff, trustees, and alumni of Whitworth University.

For their great help in this project—Sylvia Hedrick, Greg Orwig, Terry Mitchell, Jack Burns, Scott McQuilkin, Ken West, Em Griffin.

For leading me—John Thatcher, Chuck Boppell, Jim Singleton, John Young, Ed Butterbaugh, A. Blair Helman, Phil Clement, Glenn Heck, Orley Herron, John Huffman, Woody Strodel, Terry Pickett, Gordon Loux, Jack and Theo Robinson, Jim and Annette Carmean, Ed and Nancy Robinson, and most of all, Paul and Lillian Robinson.

For special support during this project—Lar, Pat, Dave, Ron, Ken, Steve, Boyd, Shakey (and their great families), the president's cabinet, my Whitworth basketball friends (just the ones who pass me the ball), Rich, Don, Chris, Terry, and most of all, Tom Robinson.

For Brenna, Ben and Bailley—the amazing grace of God.

INTRODUCTION

I don't have a grand metaphor for what I mean by "leading from the middle." I don't picture a leader like that glorious goose in the front of the V, leading its gaggle in formation to their destiny, interrupting century-old migratory patterns only to loiter on golf courses or make deposits on clean cars. The soccer match of four year olds doesn't work either. Picture the lifeless ball as the leader, always in the middle of the pack, always getting kicked around by little people. I admit that sometimes it feels that way, except the kickers aren't little.

Over the course of this book, it will become clear that my understanding of leading from the middle refers to influencing your group from *among*. I do not find leadership exercised from above, below, in front of, or from a cell phone to work as well as shoulder to shoulder. Leading from the middle refers to positioning ourselves alongside those whom we've empowered. It refers to the non-aloof ways in which leaders should see themselves. It refers to *living* in the center of a mission, rather than simply lifting it up. Using a term from Christian theology, leading from the middle refers to leadership that incarnates the mission. The Christian story is that God chose to lead a fallen human race to redemption by taking on human form and "dwelling among us" (John 1:14 NIV). I've written a book entitled *Incarnate Leadership* (Robinson 2009) that looks at the way Jesus led his disciples after pitching his tent in the middle of their camp.

I have found from studying the history of leadership, as well as from my own experiences, that leading from the middle is a very effective way for leaders to think about their styles and strategies. Proximity *to* your people and trust *from* your people go hand in hand.

William P. Robinson

PERSPECTIVE

I consider myself a student-practitioner of leadership, with the emphasis on practitioner. I did doctoral work in the area of organizational leadership and communication, but I am not what you would call a leadership scholar. I am also not a Fortune 500 leader. But I do have a sound theoretical foundation, and I have seen profound organizational changes take place in almost twenty-five years as a college president. I think my ideas might be for those to whom Joseph Rost (a first team, all-conference scholar in leadership studies) laments: "In other words, though practitioners read the leadership definitions of these scholars and study their models of leadership, they find it almost impossible to integrate and synthesize a clear, consistent picture of what leadership is and how leaders and followers actually engage in leadership" (1991, 180).

Probably the most compelling qualification for me to talk about leadership is that I've become a more effective leader over the years. I've used my background in the behavioral sciences to understand my experiences as a college president. Both theoretically and practically I've learned how to engineer leadership change.

CAN'T, CAN, MUST

First, you *can't* lead the way I lead. You wouldn't want to, and the people you lead wouldn't want you to either. The best leaders lead from their strengths. You want to lead in the way that works best for you. Only I can lead my way, and sometimes it's pretty bizarre. According to a fund-raising consultant, I'm not very presidential. I consider this high praise.

We have to work within our basic dispositions to be effective. Unfortunately, a lot of parents, coaches, and inspirational speakers try to get us to believe otherwise. Commencements are breeding grounds for these aggrandizing lies, and it's the speakers who are doing the lying. All across America eager graduates hear, "You can do anything you want to do if you really put your mind to it." No, you can't. In fact, there are a lot of things you can't do. But what graduation speaker wants to stand up and say, "Congratulations, you've run the course, you've finished the race, you've borrowed enough money to buy Wyoming, and now, just remember, no matter what anyone tells you, you're not going to be very good at a lot of things."

You can only use the tools in your kit. You can perfect them and even use them differently. But you have to be you. Leaders who force themselves to use an alien style or technique will not be effective. The best leaders know what they can do well and what they can't do well. They know the strengths and weakness of their personalities. They blend the effective leadership behaviors they learn from others into their own repertoire; they don't try to be someone they're not.

Second, you *can* change. That we have to work within our basic dispositions does not mean we can't change. If we're too timid we can become more aggressive; if we talk too much we can become better listeners; if we're too quick, we can become more deliberate. Personality theorist George Kelly observed that we are neither prisoners of our history nor our heredity (1963, 13). Where I work, my job is to lead the process of transforming young people. I don't mean this in the James MacGregor Burns's sense of transformation that you will read about in this book. I'm talking about what happens in the lives of college students during their years of living and studying with us at Whitworth. Building on the personality and gifts they bring to campus, these students blend information, values, and practices into their lives, producing staggering change. Change happens.

In several of Tom Peters' leadership books, he makes reference to Weaver Popcorn of Van Buren, Indiana. When I was president of Manchester College, I knew the Weaver family well. Their company is extraordinarily successful, thanks to the leadership that was provided by the late Welcome Weaver, former president and board chair, and by his son, Mike Weaver, who became CEO. I met Mike in 1986. At the time, he was a devoted fan of the "in-your-face" Indiana University basketball coach, Bob Knight, and a couple of his employees mentioned to me that it showed. Because of some deep personal and professional reflection, Mike decided to change the way he and the company would view the Weaver Popcorn employees. The change was authentic and penetrating. Both Mike and the company were transformed. Mike is still Mike, but he sees his world through a different lens. Employees shook their heads in disbelief at Mike's change. It is my intention to provide the theory and application that can lead to a Mike Weaver-type change.

Third, leaders *must* be people of integrity. The gist of this book is taking what we have learned about leadership over the past hundred years and building the most useful concepts into a working skill set. You could infer from this book that the acid test of a concept's usefulness is whether it works. You could assume that I lay my sacrifices on the altar of pragmatism. Such is not the case. On issues with moral dimensions, I have conditioned myself to look above the bottom line. My parents were models of this virtue, and on all things ethical, I still look up to my three older siblings who took the lead of our wonderful parents and have each followed the call to ministry. My moral foundation finds its origin in the Christian faith. I believe the Bible to be reliable and true. And I am not judgmental of those who believe differently. But I won't compromise on my conviction of what direction is true north.

In the pages that follow, I have attempted to highlight and apply important findings in this relatively new field of leadership. I have not, however, tried to suppress my own opinions. It is through the eyes of my experience that I interpret theoretical concepts. To feign total objectivity is neither honest nor enjoyable in this kind of writing exercise. And I hope readers will find both honesty and joy on every page.

LEADERSHIP DEFINED

To say the least, the definition of leadership is a moving target. A hundred years ago, we just had leaders. "Leadership" hadn't even found its way into the dictionary until the late 1800s. When it did, "leadership" simply referred to the qualities and actions of a leader. Now, by some definitions, it doesn't matter whether you serve as the mayor or the village idiot, you can still provide leadership. This book will trace the twentieth century progression of how we think about leadership. But I'll warn you, we still haven't got it figured out very precisely.

I have a friend named Jack Burns. He's a professor and a scholar in the field of leadership. (Jack is refreshing because he knows the difference between being a scholar and being an expert. Many scholars consider themselves experts. And I considered myself an expert on teenagers until I had three of my own ransacking our house. Most of the studies in Section II were conducted by "experts.") According to Jack, his field has not come up with a commonly accepted definition of leadership. It is amazing that an entire field of study can't even agree on what it is they're studying. Joseph Rost feels leadership scholars are in definitional disarray. In *Leadership for the Twenty-First Century*, he reports that in examining 587 studies on leadership he found 221 definitions (Rost 1991, 44). Apparently, the other 366 thought the definition to be self-evident. It's hard not to get the feeling that, similar to the beholders of beauty, leadership is in the eye of the led.

Jack published a long article, "Defining Leadership: Can We See the Forest for the Trees?" in *The Journal of Leadership Studies* (Burns 1996). In the article, he wove together the definitions of several leadership titans—notably James MacGregor Burns, Ronald Heifetz, and Joseph Rost—in an attempt to find some kind of big picture of leadership. In general, Jack likes James MacGregor Burns's idea of leadership as the process of transforming the attitudes and behaviors of the group. This transformation requires both the leader and the followers to adapt themselves in order to accomplish the goal.

This evolved concept of leadership is not exactly the way Teddy Roosevelt thought about it when he was leading the Rough Riders up San Juan Hill at the end of the nineteenth century. During the last hundred years, the trend of leadership in America has moved steadily *away* from the person in charge. So, can the person in charge still lead? Absolutely. But leadership no longer finds itself exclusively in the front; rather, leadership is now exercised from a full 360-degree angle. That's why "leading from the middle" is where the leader wants to be.

My working definition of leadership is pretty simple. I define leadership as an extraordinary influence that finds its source in a person or group. First, we all exercise influence of some kind. If our influence is ordinary, that's life, not leadership. Second, extraordinary things happen that alter the flow of events. Leadership occurs when a person or group, rather than some external force, causes the extraordinary to happen. Does that mean Hitler meets my definition of a leader? Yes, but his brand of leadership screams for an adjective—"heinous" gets close. Any leadership theorist who builds virtue into his or her definition of leadership makes "bad leadership" an oxymoron; unless by "bad" one means "no leadership." Furthermore, defining leadership as necessarily good defies our normal vernacular, which I will say more about in Section II. I can't argue that my definition of leadership is the best one, but it's the one I assume in this book.

GOAL

I have made no attempt to write "The Five Steps to Leading," or "Leadership Made Simple." I agree with H.L. Mencken, who said, "For every complex problem there's a simple answer, and it's wrong." Leading is not simple, but it can be done effectively by everyday people. I've written for those people, the ones who are responsible for helping groups in their efforts to accomplish important and challenging tasks.

I suppose this book will be *most* helpful to people who find themselves holding rather significant supervisory responsibilities, largely because that's my vantage point when I look at the leadership enterprise. I make the assumption that the reader occupies a position from which leadership is needed and expected. Having learned much from leaders outside my field, I think the ideas in this book will hold value beyond the world of education, even though that's my world.

I should also add that my observations will make more sense to the reluctant leader than to the ambitious one. My first performance review in my current position contained an interesting quote from a faculty member: "He loves Whitworth more than he loves being its president." No higher compliment could have been bestowed upon me. I'm at Whitworth because I absolutely love the place. I'm its president because "college president" is what I do (much more than who I am). I never planned to do this kind of work. I slipped into the role at a relatively young age, and I failed in several attempts to slip out. I was suckered into applying for the position when two my demons of my youth, Overconfidence and The-Need-For-Recognition, conspired with a personal restiveness about our living situation. After a few years, I considered returning to faculty life, but I discovered through a couple of instant rejections that not too many faculty clubs have revolving doors.

Sometimes I feel I'm on "the road I should not have taken." In my opinion, I'm a better teacher than president. And my dad was right: I don't particularly like responsibility. But my parents also instilled in me a sense of pride that makes me want to do what it takes to be the best president I am capable of being. Certainly, there are parts of the job I like very much. All I'm saying is that you'll find my ideas especially helpful if you've been cast into leadership rather than held it as a lifelong dream. Maybe it's because I backed into this job that I feel no loyalty to the conventions of being a college president. In fact, I've often felt that anyone who aspires to be a college president is probably too stupid to do the job.

SECTION I: TWENTY-FIRST CENTURY LEADERSHIP

In the twenty-first century, strong leaders will be back in favor, but the good ones will be different from their twentieth century predecessors. They will stand in a different place and use a different set of skills. In this section, I will look at how large, small, and even tiny organizations will become more federated. This decentralization of power and sometimes location will produce the need for paradoxical leadership. Consistency will be far less important than adaptability. Good leaders will spend most of their time in the middle of the action, while sliding deftly back and forth between polar opposites in style. They will be laid back and aggressive, strong and vulnerable, caring and cold-blooded. They will know the paradoxes of their positions and navigate them well. The twenty-first century leaders will also develop other qualities—some because of the federated structures of their organizations and others because of societal needs.

SECTION II: LESSONS FROM TWENTIETH CENTURY APPROACHES TO LEADERSHIP

The second section explores earlier iterations of today's most effective leadership models and attributes. In so doing, the section traces an interesting trend in leadership over the past hundred years. In the early part of the century, leadership was thought to be a quality rooted in the personalities of those who were chosen to lead—leaders were born, not made. By the 1970s, leadership had inched so far away from the personality of the leader that theorists were writing "leader" on the nametag of anyone in the group who performed acts of leadership. The twentieth century systematically decentralized leadership away from the office of the leader by spreading it across the organization. This decentralization of leadership should shock no one. During that same period, organizations moved from very centralized and hierarchical structures to more decentralized, flatter models. The history of business in the twentieth century will be characterized as decentralized. Section II traces this history of leadership through three overlapping stages without assuming, as do many leadership theorists, that each stage corrects the errors of periods gone by. A great deal can be learned by discussing the most seminal and enduring findings from each of the three eras.

SECTION III: CHANGING THE WAY WE LEAD

Without a doubt, the most frequently asked question in the field of leadership is some variation on the issue of whether leaders are born or made. In this section, I put on my behavioral scientist hat and argue that leaders can be made. People can and do change. In the 1970s, a couple of researchers at the University of Illinois set out to explain why attitude change was so unpredictable (Fishbein and Ajzen 1975). Their findings led to an understanding of what I believe are the basic components of behavior. I cast these components as steps for changing our behavior. These steps work, whether we're trying to change the manner in which we treat subordinates or trying to change our diet. In fact, people who go through dramatic behavioral change go through these steps, whether they know it or not.

REFLECTIONS

From 1996 through 1999, I managed to squeeze two study weeks into the summers. Each exquisite day, I read, wrote, and thought about life and work while sitting at our getaway place on the Pend Oreille River. Occasionally, I recorded my reflections on what I had been learning. Without necessarily intending it, I gave these thoughts the form of leadership lessons. Because many of these reflections seemed relevant, I have tucked them here and there throughout the book.

SECTION I

TWENTY-FIRST CENTURY LEADERSHIP

In the summer of 2000, we sent our kids—ages twenty-two, nineteen, and sixteen—to Europe for a summer. One night, I received a call from them informing me that they had left Budapest so that they could arrive in Prague early the next morning, which, apparently, is the best time to get into a youth hostel or a no-star hotel. For a month, they had finessed their way across southern and eastern Europe, communicating with us daily through whatever technological device was cheapest. Working the technology system is like riding a bike for these kids. During their trip, I ran into a high-school senior who said, "Hey Bill, I got a call on my cell phone yesterday. It was your Ben, calling from Barcelona." Ben could act like a big shot for fifty cents. Managing the cultures didn't pose too many problems for our young travelers, either. They are sensitive and fearless. Borders, boundaries, and distance function as details of minor consequence for their generation.

So, why did we send our kids to Europe with only Eurorail passes, a very loose itinerary, and one rule—communicate with us somehow everyday? One reason was to help them develop twenty-first century navigational tools. They are citizens of a very different world than the twentieth century one that their parents understand. In 1999, Thomas

Friedman claimed that globalization and technology have ushered in a new era. In *The Lexus and the Olive Tree* he makes his point by citing a full page Merrill Lynch advertisement that ran in all the major newspapers on October 11, 1998 (Friedman 2000, xvi). The title of the ad read, "The World is 10 years old." Five years later (age fifteen for the world) his book *The World is Flat* described an astonishing level of global parity that technology and geopolitics are bringing us at a breathtaking pace (Friedman 2005).

Organizations big and small in the twenty-first century will differ in a host of ways from their forbears, but I suspect no changes will rival the magnitude of impact caused by globalization and technology. Leadership needs will inevitably undergo changes as direct and indirect forces of globalization and technology bend the old organizational rules. This claim is not exactly a news flash, but not everyone knows how to respond. As a rule, you can get kicked just as hard by overreacting to technology changes as you can by being late. I heard about a university library that, in the early eighties, crowned microfiche as the technology of the twenty-first century, then dropped several million dollars on a massive conversion. Oops.

Over the course of the twentieth century, scholars asked four fundamental questions as they saw leadership move from the big office on the top floor to every person in the organization. Their questions are still worth asking:

- What are the traits found in the most successful leaders?

- What leadership styles seem to be most effective?

- Are there situations in which some styles work better than others?

- What kind of leadership can transform an organizational culture into one in which every person exercises leadership?

In this section, I have suggested contemporary answers to those four questions. Although I find moderation rather boring, I have tried to avoid the extremes of being too hip about the future or too romantic about the past. No one can foretell the magnitude of change that awaits organizational life, but the trends seem clear and the most effective leaders will get out in front of them.

So, what will twenty-first century leadership look like when it arrives? Joseph Rost published a book in 1991 entitled *Leadership for the Twenty-First Century*. Among his many points, two are made relentlessly. First, we don't have an agreed-upon or adequate definition of leadership. Second, what we do have suffers from the anachronistic assumptions of an industrial paradigm. Rost's insightful critique concludes by calling for a postindustrial paradigm. Unfortunately, Rost doesn't detail exactly what the postindustrial paradigm looks like. He does, however, deliver a postindustrial definition of leadership. Leadership, for Rost, is "an influence relationship among leaders and followers who intend real changes that reflect their mutual purposes." Rost defends the postindustrial nature of his definition in claiming, "This paradigm shift is massive and is immediately evident from the complete separation of leadership from management inherent in the definition," (1991, 126-7). That separation works better on paper than in practice. The fastest way to screw up your leadership is to manage badly.

I cite Rost as prologue to a couple disclaimers. First, I'm still looking for details about that postindustrial paradigm. I can be convinced to bid farewell to industrial society, but I know that we still have to make stuff. Not everybody can sell insurance or be a webmaster. It remains to be seen if Rost's postindustrial leadership ideas will work all that well in manufacturing enterprises. Second, I agree that leadership and management are two different activities. But I rather dislike leadership theorists' condescending tones when they spell out its difference from management. In everyday life, leaders without management savvy or skills will discover their leadership house is built on sand. Good management comes less easily to me than leadership. I know this, and the people who report to me know this. So I work hard on managing. When I get sloppy on agendas, individual meetings, performance reviews, and other managerial activities, the people who report to me lose direction and my big picture gets blurred. I can't lead well without managing adequately.

THE TWENTY-FIRST CENTURY ORGANIZATION

The structure and culture of most large organizations changed dramatically in the twentieth century. And, not surprisingly, these shifts ran parallel to the changes that took place in twentieth century leadership styles. Both decentralized. Organizational structure and leadership moved decision making closer to the customer. It is impossible to understand the last century's sea changes in leadership without seeing them in the context of big shifts in organizational structure. Chapter One traces the most fundamental twentieth century change in the relationship between a company's corporate center and the points at which goods and services are delivered.

ESSENTIAL TWENTY-FIRST CENTURY LEADERSHIP QUALITIES

I have identified six qualities I believe will empower the person who leads any organization through the first part of this century. The most effective leadership in the new century will be:

- **Paradoxical:** The nimble leader who knows when to tote the lunch pail and when to lift the scepter; the leader who moves humbly among all people until it is time to step forward with unshakeable confidence and rally the people with a simple, "Let's roll."

- **Secure:** Leaders who delight so much in the accomplishments of others that they barely notice their own strong role in the success; leaders whose selflessness energizes all those around them.

- **Communicative:** Leaders who realize that silence is more deadly than it is golden, that good decisions come from good information, and that "no information" speaks volumes.

- **Inspiring:** Leaders who find their way to the sanctuary of our souls; leaders who can knit heart and mind into a compelling mandate.

- **Virtuous**: Leaders whose uncompromising goodness quietly beckons the most valuable gift that any follower gives to any leader—trust.

- **Driven and Rhythmic**: Leaders with the capacity to find their highest productivity groove, the flow of life and work in which currents work together toward personal and professional fulfillment.

In suggesting these qualities, I am assuming the leader possesses: (a) sufficient intelligence, (b) sufficient expertise in the task/enterprise that she or he is leading, and (c) a commitment to continuous learning. These three characteristics are fundamental to any leadership effort. Without them, leadership will be long on form and short on content.

CHAPTER ONE

TWENTY-FIRST CENTURY ORGANIZATIONAL TRENDS

Prophesying general directions for new-century organizations poses less of a challenge than figuring out specific destinations. But the early twenty-first century does reveal some pretty clear movements. Most organizational trends evolve in the private sector, get copied by the not-for-profits, are forced upon public enterprises, and eventually show up in informally affiliated groups. Generally, these trends undergo contextualizing of some kind in order to make them fit the situations, but they still push their way into an outfit's operations or culture. For example, the service campaign of the 1980s, given display by companies such as Nordstrom and Scandinavian Airline Systems, found its way into hospitals, schools, government, and every other customer-dependent line of work (except toll booths). So the trends we see in the business organization will, ultimately, affect all organizations in some form.

THE CHARACTERISTICS OF TWENTY-FIRST CENTURY ORGANIZATIONS

I see many fads and directions in today's organizations, but four solid trends seem like pretty sure bets to last well into the twenty-first century. These characteristics are neither new nor exclusive properties of this era. They are simply organizational traits that we will see with greater frequency and magnitude. I believe businesses will become more federated, adaptive, value-driven, and connected.

Trait 1. Federated. In the summer of 2000, I enjoyed a dinner in Seattle with a friend of mine who worked for three different companies—Ma Bell, Ameritech, and Southern Bell—all without leaving his employer. Having lived through the government breakup of Bell Telephone and the SBC takeover of Ameritech, this forty-something man now had the responsibility of setting up a business for SBC in Seattle. After peppering him with questions, I concluded that the principal resources this new business would receive from the parent company were start-up capital and organizational culture. Certainly, the company brand would add to this venture, but for the most part, my buddy was building a business that would run on its own engine after being launched from the parent company.

One hundred years ago, organizations varied in size and substance, but in structure and culture they were all pretty tall and tight. Over the course of the twentieth century, many large companies decentralized in ways that brought business closer to the points of product delivery. For the most part, these regional centers were small versions of the parent company. They took orders from headquarters and tried to hit their numbers. In the past twenty-five years, however, a subtle but profound change took place. Leaders in some of the best companies in the world began to recognize that they had organizational service upside down. Profits were created in the units, not in the corporate centers (except in the scandal-ridden outfits where crooks cooked books). So, the idea of the units serving the center had to be flipped. The center began to see its central purpose as serving the units. These decentralized organizations that built unit-driven policies, cultures, and structures functioned as small federations.

It's possible this trend toward federation, more than the other two trends, is correlated with an organization's size. But even small organizations will locate responsibility and authority farther from the center and closer to their dispersed customer bases than they once did. During my graduate studies, I conducted a few research projects in network analysis. (Back then, "network" enjoyed the stable life of a noun. Now in its frenetic life as a verb, it races around trading business cards and suggesting that we *do* rather than *eat* lunch.) Because my primary interest focused on the conditions under which centralized and decentralized networks proved most effective, I have always looked at organizations on this continuum. But "federated" provides a more apt description of this trend than "decentralized." Charles Handy penned a wonderful chapter on federated organizations in his book, *Beyond Certainty,* that helps explain the difference (1996, 33-56).

Handy points out that in most decentralized organizations, the center retains all the control, delegating jobs, responsibility and even authority to the outer units. In a federated organization, the units function more autonomously, with the center providing only what the units can't effectively or efficiently do for themselves. It is like the states granting powers to the federal government, rather than the other way around. Units make their own decisions in most operational matters, yet in comprehensive organizational concerns, the balance of power tilts in the direction of the center. Handy notes that the corporate center exists to coordinate, not to control (1996, 43). For this reason, he argues that federalist centers should always be small, if not minimal. Federations are held together by trust, interdependence, and common goals. Group members hold dual citizenship in both the subsidiary and the federation.

In the twenty-first century, globalization will make federations desirable, while technology will make them possible. Staying involved with a geographically dispersed customer base will not stand in the way of close communication and feedback within the federation. Technology will allow workers to be in touch with each other while being "out there" with customers. Furthermore, employees' proximity and engagement with the constituencies they serve will turn those orders from headquarters into the famous last words of companies who don't listen to the folks on the front lines. I should also mention that organizational federalism will surface not only in the sprawling multinational corporations but even in small groups. Wherever we find independent group members or units, held together by a mutual mission rather than structural cords, we find a federated environment. This authentic distribution of rights and responsibilities alters irreversibly the relationship between the leader and the led. Central powers become more limited, and the roles of the leader become ones of coordinator, strategist, resource broker, vision builder, motivator, and encourager.

Perhaps federalism will prove to be the basic organizational model of the twenty-first century, maybe even Rost's post-industrial paradigm. For that to happen, more than structures will have to change. Warren Bennis comments, "The most practical solution, particularly for large corporations, is federalism. Federations work better than monolithic organizations because, along with strength, they offer flexibility. They are more nimble and adaptive. They have all the inherent advantages of being big but all the benefits of being small" (Bennis 2001, 159). Federalist thinking must replace the policy-driven, hierarchical patterns of thinking. Questions such as "What would the center want me to do?" will get shoved aside by "What is the best thing to do?" I think that day is upon us. In political history, federalism usually comes about by revolution. Textbooks aren't exactly littered with examples of voluntary federalism, as Handy points out. But globalization, technology, corporate mergers, fluid and disperse markets, and the demand on organizations to be both grand and personal could be the revolutionaries at the gate.

Trait 2. Adaptive. When our son was ready to go off to college, he and I built a computer; needless to say, it was a "virtual computer." Imagine a couple of technological boneheads slapping together a state-of-the-art laptop in about forty-five minutes. In all probability, no other computer in the world bore exactly the same features and specifications as the one we built. Four days later, our creation arrived at the door. The chefs at Dell had cooked up exactly what we had ordered.

Organizations that proudly decree, "If it worked in the past it will work in the future," can look forward to going under with their heads held high. Markets change and markets rule. Let's look at the computer example. I bought my first computer in 1981 after going to Sears and looking at their line. All I really needed was word processing and an electronic spreadsheet, but my choices were restricted, so my shiny, new Osborne had far more bells and whistles than I wanted. When my son Ben reached the point of buying a computer to take to college, he called the school's academic technologist and got the must-have list. After determining he wanted a laptop from Dell, he entered their website and made thirty-two decisions about features, with a running tab that calculated the cost of each choice (he owes me a lot of money). The company without the capacity to deliver exactly what Ben needed had better find lots of people my age who trust the manufacturer to guess right about what we need.

The last decade of the twentieth century will be remembered as the point in history when the emergence of technology and the proliferation of market economies joined forces to change the world. Adaptation is the only way organizations can harness, or even survive, the combustion of these two forces. Every day more people are demanding and getting what they want—right now. All organizations, not just businesses, feel the effects of immediacy bearing down on them. When I was a boy, all the Presbyterians in Itasca, Illinois, went to the Itasca Presbyterian Church. Why wouldn't they? Maybe because consumerism had not yet become a sacrament. Now they go to the place that gives them what they want. Is this bad? Not necessarily, but it does change the rules.

It will be interesting to see if our sacred cows feel the need to adapt. About a month after the terrorist attacks on the World Trade Center, I had to go to a meeting in Washington, D.C. I discovered that I could buy a round trip ticket to a D.C. airport for $1,710 or to Baltimore for $318. But I also found out that the Baltimore flight would get me back to Spokane too late for a speech I had to give. I called the United number that we high-mileage, prized customers use. I discovered that, like most post-9/11 flights, the one from Reagan National in D.C. was half full and fit my schedule perfectly. So, I explained that I worked at a college and could not justify $1,710 to go to a meeting, but I'd be willing to pay $750 to sit in one of those empty seats out of Reagan; otherwise I'd have to cancel the trip.

"I'm sorry. I can't change the fare," the agent replied.

"So you're going to throw away $750?" I asked.

"I'm sorry. There is nothing I can do," she replied.

I didn't make the trip, and United didn't make the money.

Even in running a business that trades on the tradition-rich value of the liberal arts, I deal daily with the need to make market- and technology-driven decisions. In 1986, I entered the college presidency believing that no student came to a small college out of affection for bureaucracy. I harped incessantly on the importance of being personalized in our treatment of students. In the twenty-first century, providing personal attention isn't enough. We need to move from personalized service to individualized service, and there's a difference between the two. When Ben went out to test-drive computers, all the service stores gave him personal attention—treated him like a king, actually. But when it was time to slam down the money, he demanded a product customized for his individual needs more than he demanded love and attention.

In this new century, organizations like Whitworth will inventory every service and every operation by asking two questions: Is this a point at which our mission will benefit from individualization, and does technology provide a means to individualize? The personal/individual adjustment serves as one example of the many adaptation demands that markets and technology will place on organizations.

The organization functions as a battleground for clashes between two primal human forces: resistance to change and pressure to adapt. Environmental systems work relentlessly to mold and shape us, like rushing water carves out canyons and attacks dams. Our internal defense systems fight valiantly to protect habits, predispositions, and comfort zones from all the offensives launched by our environments. As an ordered collection of individuals, the organization becomes a macrocosm of this basic conflict between inertia and external forces. With few exceptions, organizations find themselves in a Darwinian world that requires adaptation as a ticket for survival. Fortunately, this requirement often pays generous dividends. The sagacious Peter Drucker observes that "All great change in business has come from outside the firm, not from inside" (qtd. in Lenzner and Johnson 1997). In this century, organizations will adapt. The question is not whether, but how?

Trait 3. Value-driven. Last Christmas, I went to a post office to return a package that got mangled in shipping. I was told I had to go to a different post office to get an approval. I asked the attendant if she had any doubt that my request would be approved. She said no. I asked her if she had the capacity to return the package. She said yes. I asked her if she believed the sign behind her that listed customer satisfaction as the number one core value. She said yes. I said I was an unsatisfied customer, and I asked her to satisfy me by doing what she was sure the other post office would do. She said no, it was against the rules.

I asked her if she wished she worked for a company that trusted her good judgment. She didn't know what to say. I went to the proper post office. I am now an infrequent customer.

I'm a Presbyterian. This is proof positive that I'm not generally against rules. Presbyterians do things "decently and in order." We recite those words more than the Apostle's Creed. I respect rules. I obey rules. And I love competing against organizations that place rules above their values.

The twenty-first century organization that federates its structure and culture will have rules and policies, but both will yield to its core values. Over time and across situations, good judgment always outperforms a rule. Below, I've listed why I believe the best organizations will live by their values rather than die by their rulebooks:

- *Values trust your employees more than rules do.* Rules take decision making out of your employees' hands. Most rules result from bad judgment. Management attempts to "keep that from ever happening again" by creating a rule. After a speech I gave in Oregon, a man told me he had worked for a huge Fortune 500 company for thirty-seven years. At the end of his career, he decided to read the company's policy manual. He noticed it had gained weight. He explained, "What I soon realized is that I wasn't reading a policy manual; I was reading a history of the company's screw ups. Every time something bad happened, they tried to prevent a repeat by creating a rule. Now the company is run by policies more than by people."

- *Rules can betray the values they were intended to protect.* A couple years ago, my wife and I attended a meeting at a Ritz-Carlton hotel. Late one evening, our friends wanted Bonnie to play the lobby piano for them. We called the hotel security to get it unlocked. When the security man arrived, he explained that earlier in the month someone had abused the piano so it was now locked in the evenings. That Bonnie had performed with the Spokane symphony less than a month earlier failed to impress. Quite politely, we reminded him that the motto of the Ritz-Carlton is

13

"Ladies and gentlemen serving ladies and gentlemen."
He agreed. We then asked if we looked like ladies and
gentlemen. He agreed again, but said he had no choice.
The rules are the rules. And the rule ended up blocking a
gentleman from serving ladies and gentlemen. Finally, after
a full hour, the manager's manager recognized the heart
of their values was being imprisoned by a rule meant to
honor that value. Fundamentally, the hotel had elevated a
temporary rule above its most celebrated value.

- *Rules carry a tone of what **can't** be done; values zero in on
what **should** be done.* Rules stake out the boundaries,
the lines that shouldn't be crossed. Organizations need
those boundaries. But a rule-driven community tends to
be defined by its boundaries or rules, rather than by the
values those rules protect. When that happens, its identity
becomes who it *is not* rather than who it *is*. For example,
how do we think of the Amish community? By their rules—
which are no cars, no violence, and no electricity. But after
the horrifying 2007 murders of five little school girls in
Lancaster County, Pennsylvania, we saw the heart of the
Amish values, not the rules. Before they had lowered five
hand-crafted wooden caskets into the ground, they began
the difficult work of forgiving the murderer and starting a
fund to aid his widow and three children. The world that
knew the Amish only by their rules was shocked by their
hearts—hearts that revealed them to be more about love
and forgiveness than horses and buggies.

We want our organizations to be branded by their
core values, not by what they won't do. We want those
branded values to be magnets. Just before giving a speech
in Portland, Oregon, I discovered the suit I'd picked up at
the cleaners was only half my suit. The pants, I later found
out, were those of a Spokane policewoman. I had only one
hour and one hope—Nordstrom. I shot to the store where
two clerks and a tailor vowed I could walk out in a new
tailored suit in thirty minutes. They did it in twenty-five.

Nordstrom is known for the way they serve, not for making sure you follow the rules on returning an item.

- *Value-based cultures develop good decision makers.* At Whitworth, we believe that one of the most important ways we develop our students is by helping them become good decision makers. For that reason, we have as few rules as possible. Every rule reduces decision making to obedience or disobedience. Discernment is unnecessary. In place of rules, we train a large team of student-leaders in ways to come alongside their peers with guidelines and support for making good decisions. Truly service-oriented organizations understand how value-based decisions outperform rules. When a retailer, for example, trains its sales people to make decisions in the direction of its customers, it doesn't need to take on the impossible task of anticipating a rule for every possible situation. Through feedback and support, the quality of decisions will improve over time.

- *Rules often set the bar too low.* Rule-driven organizations allow members to focus on minimum requirements. Values never suggest minimum standards. In the Sermon on the Mount, Jesus illustrated this: "You have heard that it was said to the people long ago, 'Do not murder, and anyone who murders will be subject to judgment.' But I tell you that anyone who is angry with his brother will be subject to judgment." (Matthew 5:21,22) The rule is, don't murder. The value is, don't get angry. The value set a higher bar than the rule. And if you get the value right, the rule is unnecessary.

Rules are essential. They bring order, consistency, and discipline to an organization. They also represent the most efficient way to conclude a matter. I'm not anti-rules. I just think they can stunt the growth of an organization and its people. We make rules for children. As they mature, we give them more choices. Good organizations rely on the maturity and judgment of their people. They hire good people, train them, and trust their judgment.

Trait 4. Connected. Few people need to be convinced that the organizations in this new century have reached extraordinary levels of connection. The web of communication reaches in all directions. Business organizations have expanded connections with employees, customers, parent companies, research firms, and consultants. Non-business organizations also boast internal and external networks that provide members with helpful information. Organizations of all sizes need to assess their connection capacity and their communication effectiveness. We can't stay competitive and, in most cases, we can't accomplish our missions with weak message exchange systems.

Technology has eliminated all of our excuses for not communicating. Recently, we received a phone bill with what we believed were inaccurate charges. When I spoke with the phone company representative, he explained that the service we purchased didn't include certain types of operator-assisted phone calls. I maintained composure until I pointed out that we weren't told about operator-assisted calls and he grunted, "You should have known."

"Scott," I responded, "I'm your customer. Your representative left out information in selling me a service. There's no excuse for that. You could have e-mailed me, faxed me, called me, or read me the terms. You had many options, but saying 'You should have known' is not one of those options. You will lose my business and I will be an eloquent critic of your company if these charges are not removed."

Contrast this experience with a drugstore order I made over the Internet. After I filled my basket and clicked "Purchase," I heard that guy inside my e-mail system say, "You've got mail." The e-mail listed my items and provided a link I could click on if there were any errors in the order. And, as a matter of fact, I amended the order after changing my mind.

Because organizations will reach such high levels of connectivity, much of their success will depend on how well they maintain their networks. Overuse, under use, and misuse pose equal threats. The old Marshall McLuhan aphorism that "the medium is the message" may be hyperbole, but it makes a pretty good point. Our abounding connections need to stay supple and in good working order. The "when," "how," and "which" connection questions become vital in environments of virtually unrestricted information flow. You can't get sloppy in your communication practices. In my work group, the president's cabinet, we have chosen to proscribe criticisms by e-mail. It's too easy to fall into the trap of "If you can't say something nice, send it by e-mail."

Connection is in and distance is out. The organization of the twenty-first century had better know how to deal with that reality.

TWO OTHER TRENDS

Most organizational theorists could round up a half dozen or more twenty-first century trends that fall into the obvious category. My big four—Federated, Adaptive, Value-driven and Connected—seem drop-dead certain to me, but I've included them because of the direct impact they have on leadership. The two characteristics listed below will likely be smaller waves to hit the organizational beach. I suspect they will exercise a less-direct influence on the formula for successful leadership, but they will certainly influence the cultures of our organizations.

Pedagogical: For the past several years, the Korn-Ferry search firm reported a sharp rise in the number of chief learning officers they're being asked to find. These executives scan their organizations for knowledge deficiencies and then provide employees with the best learning resources. The term we keep hearing in the business literature is "the learning organization." It may take some time to determine what this term actually means, but clearly organizations failing to tap into the knowledge explosion are tomorrow's dropouts.

Meaningful: Social seismologists find our most venerated institutions on shaky ground. The stability of marriage, family, church, and even the Moose Lodge is being attacked by alternative choices. Although people have seemed willing to declare bankruptcy on their souls, they're less enthusiastic about losing their property (Machiavelli is getting smarter with each century). This trend, I believe, has created a cavernous spiritual vacuum. What else can explain the torrents of interest that have nudged spirituality beyond serious business to big business? As our inner longings deepen, people's desire for the workplace to be more than a source of income will grow. They will seek meaning and fulfillment from the organization that employs them and from the voluntary groups they join.

William P. Robinson

THE BIG QUESTION MARK

At the heart of the leadership challenge there lies a fundamental question about the twenty-first century organization that goes beyond leadership: *Will organizations return to being servants of their people, or will people continue to serve their organizations?* Every organization ever formed began as a tool for people to accomplish something. Some person, or collection of persons, felt forming an organization would enable them to do more than could be done by individuals. The organization served those who formed it as an instrument for achieving a common purpose. But somehow, for some reason, over some period of time, most organizations take on a life of their own, and the people become the servants of the organizations. I'm not sure whether this inversion is a good or bad thing. While some have welcomed the stability of "serving the organization," others have battled the intransigence of companies that have institutionalized "the way our company does business." To date, nobody has figured out how to reinvent mature organizations on a monthly, quarterly, or yearly basis, so it is not surprising that most big businesses have held their people in servitude.

In the twenty-first century, we will have the tools to return organizations to their early roles as servants. Will we run our organizations, or will our organizations run us? I suspect leaders of all organizations will face the challenge of whether and how to take on this question. It is the cosmic question of change. It is the question of who owns whom.

CHAPTER TWO

PARADOXICAL LEADERSHIP

I know a guy who almost became just the right leader. He's an uncompromising fellow, and for that I commend him. He bellied up to a nasty situation and took a lot of shots as he exposed wrongdoings. I admired him for his courage. I've been a dartboard on occasions myself, and it's no fun. Unfortunately, this person's leadership drive crashed after failing to negotiate a turn. He had gotten into a complex situation that required paradoxical leadership. Any lasting solution would be the product of *both* a steely eye and a conciliatory spirit. There were enough missteps for everybody to join in the guilt. The torchbearer would have to lead back and forth between firm standards and generous forgiveness. This would-be leader did fine on the steely eye and firm standards part, but he couldn't bring himself to stop scolding the folks he considered the transgressors. He couldn't deal with the paradoxical need both to raze baggage and raise hope.

Today's leaders must navigate the paradoxes found in current organizational structures. The tall and tight hierarchies of years gone by could tolerate less nimble leadership than the federated enterprises of the twenty-first century will require. Wherever people or units have been empowered, even in small organizations, the relationships between the whole and the parts, between the leader and the led, grow complex. A sense of dual authority replaces the more orderly chain of command. This complexity creates the need for adaptive leadership that often touches opposite poles, depending on the nuances of the situation.

In a federated environment, collisions can very easily occur when separate units angle their way into cross-purposes. No hope for mediation rests with the leader who shows up and delivers Rodney King's "Can't we just get along?" line; neither will the Wyatt Earp approach reconstruct productive relationships. The savvy leader will need to unearth the tension points and then traverse the paradoxical demands needed to renew productivity.

The need for paradoxical leadership rises not only from new organizational designs but also from changes in what those organizations are expected to deliver to their people. In the industrial age, workers saw their jobs as a way to meet their needs. Now, workers look for more. The most successful companies are meeting both needs and wants. My niece's father-in-law was a successful businessman who left the corporate world to attend seminary and become a pastor. In the first job he got more money. In the second job he got more meaning. When he retired, he got restless and took a third job. He's now serving up coffee and a saintly smile at Starbuck's. He didn't really have much in the way of needs, but he wanted to serve; he wanted a social system; he wanted all the freakin' coffee he could drink. This job is meeting his wants as much as it is meeting his needs. Here's where paradoxical leadership comes in. The leader who can meet both wants and needs will enjoy a more fulfilled workforce. Because wants are much less predictable than needs, the most effective leaders will shift smoothly from being a profit-driven taskmaster to a clown to a counselor to a listener to a cheerleader to any other role that pays more than a paycheck.

THE PRESIDENTIAL PARADOX

Where do we look for enlightenment on paradoxical leadership for today's federated organizations? At the risk of brash nationalism, I would suggest that a good place to start is with the greatest federation in world history: The United States of America. The framers of the Constitution set up a leadership system characterized by a concept that was just unimaginable at the time—limited powers in the office of the president. Article I stands guard against the strong-willed dictator, while Article II provides opportunities to wield forceful informal power, along with the formal powers placed under check. Clearly, the Constitution established the presidency as a job for the persuasive navigator. Congress would squash the monarch, and the people would throw out the weakling. With unparalleled genius, Franklin, Madison, and Hamilton led in the creation of a government with fluid, decentralized power. This may have been the first moment in history when one's leadership became more powerful than one's position as the leader.

I have a friend, Tom Cronin, who was a wonderful college president and remains one of the world's foremost authorities on the American presidency. He and Michael Genovese literally wrote the book on *The Paradoxes of the American Presidency* (Cronin and Genovese 1998). This engaging book, more than any other, has helped me understand the challenges of twenty-first century leadership. I find it absolutely fascinating that the U.S. presidency offers a better laboratory now for understanding contemporary leadership than at any time in the past two centuries.

Tom and his coauthor suggest nine paradoxes of the presidency. Four of the paradoxes these authors find in the American presidency ring prophetic of the conflicting demands that most organizations will place on twenty-first century leadership. I have also presented an additional paradox that I'm certain leaders will face. Not to belabor the point, but when leaders authentically empower people or subunits, they spread authority and limit their direct influence. By definition, this distribution creates paradoxical relationships. If leadership theorists agree on anything, it is the rising demand on leaders to empower those whom they lead. Real empowerment is not simply delegation; in fact, it is almost the opposite of what we sometimes think of delegation. When one is given a task by the leader to be done for the leader, we're talking about a favor, not empowerment. Real empowerment results from endowing people or groups with high levels of independence and responsibility. People with delegated responsibility work primarily for the boss. Empowered people work primarily for the mission. And leading a group of empowered people can get complicated.

In the early decades of this century, leaders will create structures and relationships that federate power. These leaders cannot rely on the old ways of leading, unless, of course, they reach back to the two-hundred-year-old ways of leading nestled in the Articles of the United States Constitution. Of the five paradoxes below, the first four are of the United States presidency (Cronin and Genovese 1998) that will find parallels in the leadership needed for twenty-first century organizations:

FIVE PARADOXES

Paradox 1: Americans demand powerful, popular presidential leadership that solves the nation's problems; yet they are suspicious of strong centralized leadership.

The not-too-strong, strong leader. For seven years, I found myself in the vortex of this paradox. Manchester College is affiliated with the Church of the Brethren, one of America's four historic peace churches. Serving seven years as its president, I found a clear, and sometimes painful, perspective on the Church of the Brethren's historical suspicion of authority. At once, it admired and disdained strong leaders. This became clear to me when I noticed an ominous pattern. Current leaders were held in suspicion, former leaders were appreciated, and dead former leaders were venerated. Before making this observation, I felt the Brethren simply didn't happen to like any of the people in leadership. After my realization, I softened a bit, thinking maybe this peace church just enjoyed a nonballistic form of target practice. Finally, I concluded that they really wanted centralized leadership but feared centralized power. My effectiveness in this environment required both muscle and deference, and timing was everything. In an utterly implicit and unintentional way, the Church of the Brethren taught me the difference between the use of leadership and authority.

I feel the best way for leaders to manage this paradox is by using formal power as sparingly as possible, but "not never." In any group or organization, once the power decentralization occurs, any sign of retraction threatens the empowered. Leaders can learn from our system of federal government and then program or structure a system of checks and balances. I find it helpful to think of my formal power as exhaustible credit, and to consider my informal influence as a means of replenishing tolerance for the times I need to use a formal, presidential chit. Using the very efficient and readily available power of my authority when I could engage people informally to support a similar or improved outcome squanders the benefits of federalism. I use a credit unnecessarily if not detrimentally. When I take the route of building consensus on an issue, I am nourishing the general confidence people have in my perspective, thus strengthening the base of my influence.

The paradox surfaces when we recognize that occasions do arise in which leaders must not be fearful of exercising authority over the decisions for which they will be held accountable. If we avoid those situations when formal power offers the only option to do what we believe is best for the organization, our informal influence erodes. A perception of weakness settles over our leadership. Judiciously pulling rank when the situation calls for it can strengthen leadership.

Using muscle always involves risk. Group members often chant, "Stronger, stronger . . . too strong!" It takes a pretty good shot to hit that narrow space between people's desire for "stronger" and their complaint of "too strong!" Sometimes people protest out of benign ignorance. After the Whitworth board of trustees delivered one of the few decisions that lies appropriately within a board's domain of decision making, a faculty member crossly asked me, "How can they get away with that?" I didn't even understand the question. They're the trustees—that's what they do.

Authoritarian mandates that require cooperation raise the risk even higher, and the mandates had better work. "Lincoln is often criticized for acting outside the limits of the Constitution, but at the same time he is forgiven due to the obvious necessity for him to violate certain constitutional principles in order to preserve the Union" (Cronin and Genovese 1998, 6). I'm not sure the forgiveness would have been quite so generous had his efforts failed.

Leaders in this new century must be authoritative without being authoritarian. They must be forceful without forcing. The twentieth century deal was that leaders would give power in exchange for productivity and fulfillment from those being led. Leaders can't take that power back. They must lead strongly, but with the sparing use of power. St. Paul captures the paradox in explaining that we need to be "unknown, yet well-known ... sorrowful, yet rejoicing; poor, yet making many rich; having nothing, yet possessing all things ... for when I am weak, then I am strong" (1 Corinthians 6:9-10, 12:10 NIV).

Paradox 2: Americans yearn for the common person and also for the heroic, visionary performance.

The ordinary extraordinary leader. From the Brothers Grimm to our mother's lap, we have been programmed to love the commoner-king. I remember vividly when Tom Jarman, a close friend I lured from Northwestern University to become the Manchester College athletics director and wrestling coach, introduced me to his best friend, Denny. These two guys had played football and wrestled on the same team in college, with Denny going into high-school coaching and Tom into the college ranks. Denny came across immediately as a regular guy, a fun-loving, portly old jock whom I felt I'd known for years. Ten years later, Congressman Denny Hastert moved two heartbeats away from the United States presidency, serving his country as speaker of the House of Representatives. I'm thrilled that "one of us" occupies this lofty office. Only in America—on the other hand, I'm terrified that "one of us" was running Congress. Congress could have been on its own if they got tangled up in session over a weekend when "da Bears" were playing.

An obituary in *The Economist* for Spiro Agnew tells the story of a watering hole in Baltimore where a group of regulars were toasting the pedestrian views of Vice President Agnew. After their sudsy conferral of sainthood on Spiro, a journalist stunned the group by interrupting the coronation with the question of whether they'd like their man Spiro to be president. One guy's reply illustrates the commoner-king paradox: "I don't want the President of the United States to sound like me after a couple of beers" ("Spiro Agnew" 1996, 105). How does today's leader satisfy Americans' desire for leaders who are, in the words of Cronin and Genovese, "greater than anyone else, yet not better than themselves?"

My answer to this question is painfully trite, but painfully true. Leaders must come to terms with their own vulnerability. Often we talk about being vulnerable as an act of stooping, and a quite noble one for those leaders whose sweat doesn't smell bad. I can't stand it when leaders or speakers make a big deal about how they're going to be vulnerable and disclose some frailty, as if we thought they were flawless. The king side of the commoner-king paradox generally gets conferred upon leaders by virtue of their positions and skill sets. On the other hand, being a member of the commoner club requires an honest and open recognition that in so many areas we are vulnerable—just one stumble away from abject failure.

My best example of serving as commoner-king comes from a leadership position that requires daily traverses of this paradox: the cleric. My former pastor, Jim Singleton, is, at once, one of the most godly and human people I have ever met. Owing primarily to geography, our church represents a blend of professional and nonprofessional workers. When Jim took a call to another church, we were all heartbroken. Whether we marched to work with blue collars or white collars, we all felt we were losing one of us. Jim was our *commoner* because he knew, and we knew that he knew, that he just happened to be the "wretch like me" up front, using his rare gift for helping us grasp the impenetrable mysteries of a holy God. He was our *king* because his longing to know God gave honesty, eloquence, and even royalty to the ordinary. As he met the ups and downs of life, he was just like us, but somehow better, and we loved having him as our leader.

Paradox 3: Americans want a just and compassionate president, yet we admire a cunning and, at times, ruthless leader.

The tender-hearted, cold-blooded leader. If you're not leading a country, being described as ruthless might be a bit harsh. For most of us, this paradox can be thought of as tender-hearted and cold-blooded. In thinking about this paradox, it's hard not to conjure up images of the twisted morality that has the Mafia godfather roughhousing with his children in the morning and roughing up a "slow learner" in the afternoon. Actually, this paradox will unfold in quite the opposite manner in current organizational leadership. Leaders will need ice in their veins on matters of principle and morality, but they will also need understanding hearts in their human relations. They must *ruthlessly* guard personal and organizational integrity, but that resolve must be carried out with justice and compassion.

Operating at only one pole on this paradoxical continuum won't work in the future, and wasn't very effective in the past. In the early 1990s, Middlebury College in Vermont had a mess on its hands.

Evidently, their operating budget turned red, so they hired a consulting firm to help trim their payroll. They made the cold-blooded decisions that needed to be made if they were to preserve the strength and integrity of this excellent college. Unfortunately, the consultants were equally cold-blooded in executing (no pun intended) their conclusions. Pink slips and "Clear out your desk by noon tomorrow" notes violated the culture and the individual loyalty that characterized Middlebury. The consultants knew they'd made a mistake when faculty and staff arrived at commencement exercises in funeral regalia.

I've never made a really hard decision in which the victims cheered for me. But in those difficult moments of making the hard call, for some reason I felt a strong sense of compassion. I've felt this as both a leader and as a father. I recall one night when I delivered a totally arbitrary "no" to our seventeen-year-old son's request to join his friends in an inherently harmless activity, but one that I could not bring myself to approve. With tears streaming down his face, he blamed my decision on everything from me not trusting him to my need to protect my own image. Fortunately, I didn't have it in me to accept his invitation to do battle. I was too sad about what it meant to fulfill my obligation as his father. I learned a good leadership lesson that night. Because of my commitment to our son's best interests, I could not compromise this decision, nor could it matter how cruel my authoritarianism felt to him. But I ached horribly for the pain being endured by the boy who means more to me than any other male on this earth. And because I couldn't really hide my anguish, he recognized how much I hated the role of parent at that moment. We both recovered, and by the end of the night, we were laughing at the naked shamelessness with which he had tried to leverage my distress into some kind of payoff that I have now forgotten.

That night, I went to bed thankful that I'd said no with a hanging head, rather than a stiff neck. Neither the hard-heartedness of my decision nor the soft-heartedness of my response could have survived that encounter without the primal instincts of the parent-child relationship. The clear lesson of the episode was my need to consider this paradoxical integration of opposites whenever I appear in front of the most difficult of decisions. Cold-blooded doesn't necessarily mean arbitrary, but it does mean difficult. I can't back down from that.

Tenderhearted doesn't necessarily mean soft or even generous, but it always means compassionate and respectful. I violate everything I stand for if I protect myself with a cold veneer. Today's leaders must develop square jaws and soft hearts and, most importantly, must know when to lead with which.

Paradox 4: Americans want powerful, self-confident presidential leadership; yet they are inherently suspicious of leaders who are arrogant and above criticism.

The confident humble leader. No matter what you thought about Ronald Reagan's politics, you have to agree that his navigation of this paradox was masterful. No president in my lifetime exuded more confidence in his political philosophy, nor has any president in my memory seemed more comfortable in laughing at himself. This fusion of self-assurance and vulnerability may be why many people acknowledge Reagan's leadership impact even if they contest his success.

Below, I discuss the importance of personal security as an indispensable element of twenty-first century leadership. I believe security serves as one of the important ties that bind confidence and humility. Although Cronin and Genovese present the American appetite for leaders with confidence but not arrogance as paradoxical, confidence and humility dwell well together in the truly secure leader. It is exactly the strong sense of self that allows a leader to feel confident enough to get the job done and secure enough to deflect credit and welcome criticisms that improve his or her performance.

Success in developing and displaying confidence without arrogance relies heavily, but not exclusively, on a healthy self-concept. Propelling leaders' movement between confidence and humility also requires a strong and honest *self-awareness*. There are some tasks in the life of our university that I do really well. They are jobs I've done many times, and they play to my strengths. I'm the only one I want doing them, and I think my coworkers share that opinion. In most jobs around the university, however, I would find myself two standard deviations below the mean in quality of performance, and I *know* my coworkers share that opinion. It is this self-awareness that enables my colleagues to believe that neither my confidence nor my humility is false or strategic.

When former Boston Celtic star Larry Bird walked into the locker room before the first All-Star Game's three-point shooting contest, he called out, "Which one of you boys is gonna get second place this afternoon?" He then buried the competition. Larry Bird did not, however, pose that question or even enter the competition in the slam-dunk contest. The man had a love affair with gravity. Confidence and humility coexist harmoniously in leaders who know what they can and cannot do well

The federated authority of twenty-first century organizations places leader arrogance in direct conflict with the organizational structure and climate. Leaders neither can nor should do it all. They must, however, have the ability and confidence to hold together the loosely bound units through which their missions are accomplished. Strength without arrogance enables them to meet the demands of the humble/confident leader paradox.

Paradox 5: Americans expect leaders to be both visionary and realistic.

The idealist realist leader. Vision without realism is fanciful; realism without vision is depressing. Leading requires both. But most leaders get knocked for lacking vision or for being too idealistic. This paradox always seems to put a fat kid on the other side of our teeter-totter. Solomon had a good point in observing, "Without a vision, the people perish" (Proverbs 29:18 NIV). And we also accept Professor Noel Tichy's claim that "facing reality is the first crucial step that leaders must take" (Tichy and Cohen 1997, 31). Actually, these two poles aren't that far apart, which is why leaders don't have to drift very far from the midpoint before suffering the criticism of camping at one extreme or the other.

In my experience, the success of any attempt to unite vision and realism will rest on a fundamental premise—one that many failed leaders never understood. Leaders do not bring vision *to* an organization; rather, they extract a vision *from* it. Successful leaders dig into their organizations, mine the gold, and then figure out how and where to sell it. Having completed this painstaking exercise in reality, they trade in their picks and shovels for a chisel and begin to sculpt an image of what their enriched organizations can become. Bennis and Nanus are great on this point:

> In the end, the leader may be the one who articulates the vision and gives it legitimacy, who expresses the vision in captivating rhetoric that fires the imagination and emotions of followers ... But if the organization is to be successful, the image must grow out of the needs of the entire organization and must be "claimed" or "owned" by all the important actors. (Bennis and Nanus 1985, 109).

Leaders must till their organizations for the makings of an achievable ideal. The people will recognize the reality and the reach and will feel ownership of both.

We need idealism from those we lead and from those who lead us. On a recent trip to Amsterdam, our family visited Corrie Ten Boom's hiding place where she protected Jews from their voracious Nazi predators. We were gloriously inspired by acts of heroism and strength. As I listened to the stories, I found myself thinking that the superhuman acts of the stowaways were not really stories of the survival instinct; they were stories of hope. It was vision that kept the Jews from perishing in World War II. The manna of hope that they would one day embrace loved ones sustained them more than a primeval fear of loss of life and limb.

As leaders, we must provide visions that inspire hope. While visions may bound wildly about, true hope always settles within the latitudes of reality. Rare is the organization or group that exceeds the measurements of its leader's vision. But even rarer are the people who find hope in fanciful, unrealistic visions.

THREE WAYS TO TRAVERSE THE PARADOXES

I feel very strongly that paradoxical leadership will serve twenty-first century organizations better than the unbending styles that provided comfort and predictability for yesterday's less-complicated enterprises. After offering the above paradoxes, I would like to suggest three rules for traversing them:

1. Go wide. Some who read this section on paradoxical leading will claim that I'm simply putting a new spin on the need for balance, which is hardly a new thought. They're wrong. Balance is achievable through timid baby steps, back and forth between two poles. I'm campaigning for a fat standard deviation—getting way out there in both directions. When it's time to be king, don't be a wimp about it. Leave no doubt about who's running things. When it's time to be commoner, lose the symbols of your office. The minute a leader gives the impression that being commoner for a few moments is an act of magnanimity, that leader is cooked. Leaders need to cut a wide berth in all the paradoxes of their roles, being bipolar in a healthy sense of the word.

2. *Angle into the current.* I've written most of this book lifting my eyes intermittently to watch the magnificent Pend Oreille River push north toward the fabled waters of the Columbia River. When I kayak on the Pend Oreille, I am never unaware that going with the flow will turn my kayak into a magneto. Any direction but north requires intention and effort. Paradoxical leaders must know the currents of their own preferences and personalities. Rarely will they find situational eddies that move them naturally upstream. For example, with respect to the powerful but not too centralized paradox, distributing authority comes more naturally to me than wielding it. Hence, I far more frequently ask myself the question, "Where do I need to engage?" than I ask, "Where am I micro-managing?" Centralizing power and exercising authority represent upstream actions for me. So occasionally I point my kayak in that direction, assuming that the currents of my style have carried me in the direction of decentralization. Leaders need to know where their comfort points lie on the paradoxical continuums of their positions, and they must be sure that they make moves toward the farthest pole. As a rule, angle upstream.

3. *Don't become predictable.* In general, impact and predictability are inversely related. One of the great benefits of paradoxical leadership lies in the ability it provides the leader to avoid tight patterns. Leaders need to take advantage of the impact available to those who visit the poles. For the most part, distance from the opposite pole creates impact.

Once at a dinner party, I finished eating before the other folks at our table, so I gathered everyone's dirty dishes and bussed the table. A couple of visitors considered my service salutary because of the distance it represented from my normal duties as president. Although my wife would break a dish over my head if I suggested dishes weren't in my job description, I guess for these folks, the surprise created impact. In another instance I saw some surprise-based impact at the opposite pole of this paradox when some students invited me (their buddy) to participate in an activity they'd dreamed up. Not only did I decline, I explained that they too would be declining. The message that I (now less their buddy) wanted them to hear managed to get around. Leaders skilled in the paradoxes will recognize that the unexpected act packs more of a punch than the next stop in a standard pattern.

I suspect the ultimate paradox of leadership grows out the longing people have for their leaders both to follow and lead them. Knowing when to reflect (follow) and when to shape (lead) the hopes and expectations of those we lead will determine the success with which we navigate the paradoxes. Some leaders will find it difficult to climb out of the trenches created by years of leading in a particular way. Others might reject paradoxical leadership as chaotic, if not duplicitous.

When I have succeeded in arcing polar opposites, I have experienced a sense of wholeness. I am much more than someone's idea of a college president. In fact, only on the most formal of occasions am I comfortable in being addressed as anything other than "Bill." I do not wish to be narrowly known by my role or my degree. I love serious debate, and I love spontaneous laughter. I love to serve, and I love to be served. I love to teach, and I love to learn. In a sense, paradoxical leadership respects the glorious complexity of being made in the image of God. It is whole leadership for whole people.

LEADING FROM THE MIDDLE

Paradoxical leadership does not work well from a distance. A couple of years ago, I was interviewed by a pretty large national magazine in response to an award we had won for workplace climate. Oddly, the article that came out was entitled, "President in Sweats." Maybe my work uniform turned out different than what she expected. I would like to think that factors way more important than what I wear to work have contributed to our campus culture, yet the reporter somehow saw this informality as a symbol of proximity to the people (rather than the less generous but more accurate attribution of being too lazy to dress up). To my knowledge, nobody at Whitworth particularly notices what I wear. I hope it is because I'm close to our people that they aren't startled when I show up in sweats one day and a suit on the next. I hope I am close enough for them to see my sincerity, and I hope it is for that I am granted the freedom to worry more about my effectiveness than my image.

I wouldn't be surprised if paradoxical leadership comes across as nimble from leaders close to their people, and as chaotic from leaders that rule from a distance. The success of paradoxical leadership probably rests on the perceived authenticity of the leader. And we usually require a close look to see if a person's actions are genuine.

REFLECTION
Casting—Controlling Your Role

A few months after taking my place in my first president's chair, I began to wonder about my image. On the Saturday morning after classes began, I threw on some sweats, pulled a hat over my unwashed hair, hopped on my bike, and cruised over to the gym to check out our women's volleyball match. En route, I spotted an abandoned, half-consumed six-pack of beer (no doubt blown onto campus by strong winds) in a parking lot. I scooped it up and rode on. Predictably, a passerby in a car hollered, "Looking very presidential today aren't we?" Whatever it meant to look presidential, I was pretty sure I didn't.

I had decided that one of my most important tasks would be to shape a campus culture that would empower the accomplishment of our mission. What role should the president take in order to create a climate that would drive the mission? As a student of behavioral sciences, I was acquainted with the force of roles. Their power continues to astonish me. In a sudden role shift, such as getting a phone call from our supervisor while we're conversing with a subordinate, we can almost physically feel our change in persona.

As a new college president, I learned that whoever took charge of casting my role would shape the environment. I needed to understand my role repertoire and *cast myself* in the roles that were appropriate for the moment and the mission. There were many "directors" on campus. Sometimes unwittingly, sometimes intentionally, they cast me into roles that would serve their purposes. I discovered that my institutional perspective and self-awareness put *me* in the best position to choose the appropriate role. Sometimes the role I chose coincided with the ways in which others were trying to cast me; sometimes it did not. The battle was in my taking control of my self-perception.

Two discoveries followed. First, I realized that there are many roles that can be used to do a job effectively; hence, I probably worried too much about finding a correct role. As it turns out, my general approach to overseeing a college developed into one quite different from those of any of my friends who do this job. Second, my experience confirmed the theory that there is a predictable synchrony resulting from the roles we choose. Others see us in the way we see ourselves; others feel comfortable with us when we are comfortable with ourselves; others feel confident in us when we feel confident in ourselves. Our social environment takes on mirror qualities. How we see ourselves has a profound impact on how others see us. We need a mindset in which we think of our position in terms of holding the reins on roles that lead to effectiveness.

Chapter Three

Secure Leadership

Of the six leadership qualities, security and virtue probably transcend eras more than the other four. But current, less centralized organizational environments elevate the value of being secure and virtuous.

Through the ages, group members have enjoyed being led by secure people. I define a secure leader as the person motivated to meet the task and needs of the group more than his or her personal needs. I once met with a trustee to seek advice about an administrator whose leadership was proving very ineffective. At one point, the trustee looked at me and said, "You're offended by his insecurity, aren't you?"

The question caught me off guard. Offended? I responded with, "I guess I am," but I had to take that question home and think about it. She was right. I was offended that this person put meeting his needs in front of meeting those of the faculty. The first time he co-opted credit for a faculty member's accomplishments, the group cut him some slack. The second time they asked me to cut him from the team. Both times it upset me.

If we were to examine the causes of leadership failure by adding up all the bad luck, bad group members, and leaders' incompetence, the sum of the causes wouldn't come close to the number of leaders felled by their own ego needs. Ego has never been more aptly described than it was one hundred fifty years ago by Cardinal John Henry Newman: "Quarry the granite rock with razors, or moor the vessel with a thread of silk; then may you hope with such keen and delicate instruments as human knowledge and human reason to contend against those giants, the passion and the pride of man" (1852, 121).

In one of the most fascinating organizational studies ever conducted, Jim Collins introduced the world of management and leadership to the Level 5 leader. With remarkable consistency, companies that met the study's definition of greatness were led by ostensibly secure leaders. In the January 3, 2006 issue of *Management Issues*, Stuart Crainer interviewed Collins, author of this best-selling book, *Good To Great: Why Some Companies Make the Leap...And Others Don't*. When asked to define the Level 5 leader, Collins replied it came down to one essential definition. The central dimension for Level 5 is a leader who is ambitious first and foremost for the cause—for the company, for the work, not for himself or herself—and has an absolutely terrifying iron will to make good on that ambition. .Level 5 leaders live in the awareness that *it is not about them, it is for the company* and its long-term interests, of which they are just a part (Crainer 2006).

In essence, Collins found that the most successful leaders drew satisfaction from the prosperity of their companies. His study also found a higher incidence of egomaniacs in companies that failed to climb from good to great.

Insecurity surfaces at the extremes. Generally, bravado, timidity, and micro-management serve as the most visible portals of insecurity. They do not work for the leader, especially in the new organizational culture. Increasingly decentralized structures require leaders to be confident and spacious. Authority must be distributed enthusiastically, rather than cautiously guarded by the timid or lodged in the ego of the proud. Caution and egocentricity keep the leader too close to the center in the current business environment. I offer two suggestions for the leader trying to become more secure:

LET GO TO GO

I found something I wrote ten years ago that sounds like an attempt to convince myself of this principle, but it still applies, at least to me.

Leading is not about me. Letting go of my recognition, my image, my control and my self-interest will free me to grasp my responsibility. My duty is to see that this college executes its mission with excellence and strength. Any needs I have to be the star or marionette of that execution steal from Whitworth and misdirect my energy. When I let go of me, my role changes. I become the dispatcher rather than the driver, the coach rather than the player, the resource rather than the watchdog, and the interpreter rather than the expert. If I stick to my self-concept of strategist, spokesperson and inspirer, I think I can survive this job for a few more years. But if everything's all about me, I will buckle under the weight of my own frailties and needs. It's too hard to keep my ego fed. The more it gets, the more it wants.

I haven't read the book, but I heard that the first sentence in Rick Warren's best seller, *The Purpose Driven Life*, is "It's not about you" (2002, 17).

Our habits and our reflexes fake us into hanging on when we should let go. Those of us in fund-raising operations get suckered both by habits and reflexes. We work hard and deserve recognition, but our language makes it sound like we deserve as much credit as our benefactors. For example, in reporting on a capital campaign, fundraisers will tell a group of donors, "We've raised $88 million toward our goal." Do those donors want to hear how good we are, or how good they are? Why wouldn't fund-development people say, "To date, you and other friends of the college have given $88 million?"

Credit-taking language is a bad habit, formed by talking mostly to each other. But reflexes also pitch in. When fundraisers report the fruits of their hard work, it really does feel like they raised the money and that they should get kudos for their efforts. Most gifts would not materialize without their good work. So they give themselves a few pats on the back. This very act can defeat its own purpose. When we hear a self-congratulatory tone from someone, we don't need to say, "Good job"—they already took care of that. Having said all that, I know that a part of this language comes from the willingness of good, hard-working fund-raisers to accept the responsibility for reaching their goals. Good for them! I'm honored to be a card-carrying member of their tribe.

Empowering others is another area of letting go that secure leaders handle more easily than their insecure counterparts. I suspect that secure leaders delegate responsibility where insecure leaders delegate jobs. Bass makes a very interesting statement in summarizing existing research: "Delegation remains a relatively unexplored management option despite the evidence of its important contribution to organization effectiveness" (1990, 909). When I read this, I realized I have never really discussed with those who report to me directly their perceptions of their responsibilities. I can't believe I haven't done this. Do the people reporting to me feel their duties have been given to them by me or by their job descriptions and the mission of the organization? Am I secure enough to say it's the latter; that they work for Whitworth and not for me? I need to schedule a few conversations about empowerment.

The twenty-first century CEO must serve as the agent for the overall organization by empowering and equipping unit leaders to charge forward. Insecure leaders who delegate jobs while keeping a tight rein on their people will look like maypoles. Tethered people will adoringly run in circles around them, while the competition gleefully runs circles around their organizations.

ANDRE WAS WRONG

I've read numerous accounts of tennis great Andre Agassi's professional turning point coming when he stopped believing his own line that "Image is everything." If Agassi stopped believing Agassi, so should the rest of us. The third and fourth chapters of Burns's *Leadership* (1978) discuss many of the psychological factors that influence the role self-esteem plays in exercising leadership. It's an interesting, though highly inferential, presentation of the effects various psychological factors have on leaders. Burns quotes William James, who defined self-esteem as the numerator of success over the denominator of pretension. I'm not sure these two variables are best represented as a fraction, but I am sure that lowering pretense raises the odds of successful leadership.

I work in an industry that specializes in pretense. We present ourselves to American society as liberal champions of the powerless.

We demand justice and egalitarianism. But just let those powerless proletarians try addressing us without our lofty titles, and we'll drop a load of condescension on them like they've never seen before. We rank our faculty members and call ourselves doctors. Mind you, it's not pretense. We are a humble folk, seeking only to preserve respect for the positions we occupy, not for ourselves. Yikes. We're not only full of ourselves, we're dishonest about it. I appreciate the well-intentioned respect I am afforded as a university president. But there's nothing sacred about my job, and I would rather be respected for how I do it than the mere fact that I occupy the position.

Leaders must feel secure enough to quit worshipping the Baal of image. People need real leaders, not Madison Avenue creations or self-saturated potentates. What we wear, how we're dressed, the size of our offices, and how we're addressed all serve to expand or reduce the distance between ourselves and those we lead. Secure leaders work to narrow the gap.

We need to see our people and ourselves in functional rather than hierarchical roles. This perceptual shift flows in the direction of organizational trends that accent serving those we lead. Moreover, de-emphasizing hierarchy can reinforce our efforts to empower people. I have a pretty big office compared to other people where I work. One day while visiting with another college president in his palatial office, I thought "What a waste to burn all this space on presidents who are gone half the time." (I'm way better at seeing others' big offices than my own.) A couple months later, we bought the kind of workstation in which I could hide my computer, phone and junk piles, and then we converted the rest of my office into a conference room. Now, people schedule my office for meetings when I am out of town. I'm pretty sure nobody is thinking, "Well, he's not the leader I thought he was if he's willing to let people use his office."

A number of years ago, I pulled together the search committee for a very important position. I asked the members what they would choose as the most important quality we should seek. The first response was, "someone who is comfortable with him- or herself." Leaders making waves in the new century will put mission and people well ahead of meeting their own personal needs. It's not that big of a deal.

LEADING FROM THE MIDDLE

My grandfather instilled in me a love for the cello, and Anne Martindale Williams, principal cellist of the Pittsburgh Symphony since the late 1970s, is my favorite cellist in all the world. I love Yo-Yo Ma and Rostropovich, but I'd rather hear Anne. First, I hear God in her bow. Second, during my doctoral studies of organizational leadership, Anne taught me about the "middle." At that time, she, her husband Joe, and my wife Bonnie would do chamber music programs, so we were good friends. During Advent of 1979, I invited a bunch of my crazy, tone-deaf friends to come over to the house for a Christmas carol party. For these guys, the operative word in the invitation was "party." I had somehow conned Bonnie into accompanying our "chorus" and almost facetiously invited Anne and Joe to come over. "Sure," Anne replied, "should we bring our instruments?"

This woman, who spent her Friday nights four feet to the right of conductor Andre Previn, who paid three times more for her cello than for their house, was offering to cast her pearls before us musical swine who made up in volume what we lacked in talent. As I sat in our tiny living room watching her roar with laughter and play with a virtuosity that not ten other living cellists could match, I realized that she was every bit as comfortable in the middle of regular people as in the front of the Pittsburgh Symphony. Such security just magnified the power of her selflessness. When Anne was in the middle, she cared nothing of image, nothing of impressing others, nothing of anything other than giving a gift to her friends.

Today's leaders must be secure enough to be seen and known up close. They must put themselves so close to those they lead that pretense becomes impossible. When they walk into the middle, they communicate a confidence that respect is not about image and posturing. Silently, they announce they are not afraid to be known.

REFLECTION
LETTING GO

I'm convinced we can't "go" if we don't "let go." I became particularly aware of this a number of years ago when I found myself playing in a big three-on-three basketball tournament with my eighteen-year-old son, Ben, and his two eighteen-year-old friends. We were in the "18 to 24 year old, 6'2" and under" division. The tournament, Spokane's Hoopfest, has a provision that allows you to play on a team if you're so much older than twenty-four that you can't possibly help the team. I was a shoo-in on that basis, not to mention the fact that in the last year my entire body has totally crashed. I've played in the appropriate category with friends for the last five years. I love it, and I've played pretty well. But this year I was not with my peers, and in a flash of uncharacteristic maturity, I knew I shouldn't jack up a shot every time I got my hands on the ball. I had a new role, the only role that made sense, but a role that was foreign to me—tag along. It worked. The fifth wheel was the one Ben needed me to be. It was the "dad wheel." For me to excel as father, I had to let go of my self-image in basketball.

Being a parent of my dear daughters Brenna and Bailley forces me to deal with "letting go." When Brenna headed off to college, it made my eyes squirt, but I didn't have to let go of my fundamental relationship with her. However, last summer the kid hauled off and got married. With one "I do," I became the Number Two man in her life. It's different. I let go, but I got back more in exchange. I'm still her dad, and she still lies about how great I am. But now she also has a great husband, and what can make a father happier than that?

Giving up elements of our personal and professional life will free us for personal and professional growth. Not long into my current job, I had an image of our school that was destroying my objectivity. It was my picture, and I was the president, both of the picture and the university. In our institutional-planning process, I kept looking at our needs and opportunities on the canvas of my vision. I realized that for me to know if my picture was the best one for the future of Whitworth, I had to let it go. With me at its easel not too many re-paints were going to be suggested. So I backed off, people stepped up, and the result is a better picture than the one I started with. We may reach a point where I have to say, "This is how it's going to be" but it won't be before we start.

Chapter Four

Inspiring Leadership

"When Aeschines spoke, the people remarked, 'How well he speaks.' But when Demosthenes spoke, the people cried out, 'Let us march against Philip!'"

I can't remember who uttered this line, but I love it. I'm a sucker for inspiration. I don't care if leadership scholars feed inspiration to the dinosaurs; the chances of me following will skyrocket when a leader inspires.

To inspire is to propel people to action. It is to deliver a compelling vision of what could be. Inspiring relies less on authoring the vision than on being able to deliver it straight to the soul. Granted, being the visionary may add to the impact, but people can inspire on many bases other than "I thought this up." I have an African-American friend who stutters occasionally and gets a little sideways when offering spontaneous remarks. But when he launches into Martin Luther King, Jr.'s "I Have a Dream" speech, you listen with your blood. The last time I heard him give it, through my tears, goose bumps, and shame I silently vowed to march relentlessly against the "Philip" of racism.

The Greek translation of inspire is "to breathe into." The inspirational leader breathes energy and life into the people being led. Leaders in the twenty-first century will most often deliver inspiration in the form of passionately communicating how to fill the gap between what is and what could be. Both organizations and individuals must understand how to bridge the distance between the status quo and their full potential. It is not enough for leaders to point the way; they must stir the passions of those they lead. I used to love watching Don Barbieri, chairman of Spokane-based WestCoast Hospitality Corporation, when he served as CEO. He marched around the company with passion and joy. He embodied his belief that the ideal was not idealistic, that the ideal could be achieved.

James Kouzes and Barry Posner use the Greek translation of "inspire" to define this essential dimension of a leader's responsibility.

> Leaders breathe life into the hopes and dreams of others and enable them to see the exciting possibilities that the future holds. Leaders forge a unity of purpose by showing constituents how the dream is for the common good. Leaders can't ignite the flame of passion in others if they don't express enthusiasm for the compelling vision of their group. (1997, 11)

While sitting here thinking about inspiration, I heard a Scottish piper blow strains of an old hymn that stirred my memory of a dying young woman. In an astonishing act of leadership, she breathed life into those of us allowed to enter the sanctuary of her final days. Shortly after the oncologist handed Suzanne a four-to-six-weeks sentence, she built a furious to-do list, with "The Party," exactly six weeks out, at the top of her list. Suzanne had no intention of "going gentle into that good night." She would be at that party, and there was a ton to be done. So Suzanne built a program through which she would indefatigably lead us as she left us. The scene of the culminating party was a beach house in Laguna Beach, California, where she spent her final weeks.

On the afternoon of the party, Bonnie and I arrived at John Wayne Airport; we were scheduled to depart at six the following morning. The event was grand. Suzanne took control, not so much of us, but of the atmosphere from which she deftly removed both denial and misery. By two AM, exhaustion had conquered all but Suzanne, Bonnie, and me. For the next three hours, this brilliant twenty-three-year-old Princeton graduate conducted a clinic on life. As the time drew near for our final embrace with Suzanne, I asked her, "What have you learned in the last six weeks?" With the quiet confidence of a woman who had seen more of life's mysteries than most people thrice her age, she replied, "That what we learn isn't as important as what we do with what we learn."

The night before her funeral, which she had asked me to conduct, I woke up at three AM and sobbed helplessly, as I had five months earlier when we'd learned the cancer she had once beaten was back. But I did not cry when we said our final goodbye. I remember, almost with guilt, that as I held Suzanne before leaving for the airport, I felt a greater sense of duty than grief. Suzanne knew we would never see each other again, but she did not give me a teary-eyed goodbye. Without words she commissioned me "to *do* with what I've learned."

God forbid I write anything here that uses the memory of this precious woman just to make a point. But Suzanne breathed life into me. She moved us to action. She called us to be doers. Like all good leaders, Suzanne took risks, made mistakes, and failed in a few efforts as her end drew near, due partially to her lifeline of steroids. But she donned the mantle of leadership in a way that dwarfed her frailties and flaws. Suzanne, ever a leader, seized the moment to inspire, and she taught us what the word means.

Leaders today compete with complacency, distraction, and a bombardment of fingertip diversions that tug on their people. Loyalty, honor, and duty can atrophy beneath the fast-paced tedium of simply keeping up with life. But when we breathe energy into these dormant virtues, people will rise to the specifications of our vision. They will "march against Phillip."

LEADING FROM THE MIDDLE

People who lead from the middle are able to inspire not only with their messages, but also through their lives. I worked for a provost named Glenn Heck. He was brilliant. His throwaway comments were better than most people's best orations. Almost everything he said inspired me. Glenn made no effort to distance himself from those of us who reported to him. We knew him well, and he knew us well. Quite by coincidence, but because we were so close to Glenn, I learned about an incredibly sacrificial gift that he and his wife had very quietly made to their church. The discovery utterly astonished me. It added moral authority to everything Glenn had spoken. For most of us, our ability to inspire rests more in the way we go about our work and live our lives than in our rhetorical skills. St. Francis is said to have urged his followers, "At all times preach the gospel, and when necessary, use words."

REFLECTION
MY BAD

I play basketball several times each week. It's good exercise, and it reminds me of something I used to do well. In basketball, there's a floor language to which all players are privy and that no nonplaying spectator could imagine. One of the most frequent utterances on the court follows an error in judgment when the guilty party mourns, "My bad." This admission is particularly forthcoming when there could be some argument over whose bad it really was. For example, a stolen pass can be thrown too softly or to the wrong side of the receiver. However, if the receiver doesn't move toward the ball as it is thrown, it gives the defender the split second needed for a steal.

"My bad" immediately prompts the confessor into (a) working harder to make up for his or her "bad," (b) concentrating on not making the same "bad" again, and (c) showing the team he or she takes responsibility for a mistake. All of these things are good.

I think people in leadership have to form a "my bad" mental reflex that kicks in whenever there's a problem. Whether we're thinking in terms of our organization or ourselves, we must ask what we could have done better. I remember sitting with two angry parents who felt their children had been ill treated at one of our co-curricular activities. At one point I mused, "It doesn't sound to me like we handled that particular situation very well." I was almost thinking out loud to myself. What followed was interesting:

1. The parents softened, and we had a more objective discussion.

2. I later spoke with the overseer of that co-curricular area to see if, indeed, we hadn't handled the situation very well.

3. I discovered we had dealt with the student in a reasonably supportive way, but the supervisor and I did find a couple areas in which we fell short of the ideal.

4. The supervisor decided to discuss in general this shortcoming at their department retreat.

5. I saw the student in question, and I worked hard to make up for what might have been a weakness in our handling of this situation.

One "my bad" produced at least five "goods."

CHAPTER FIVE

COMMUNICATIVE LEADERSHIP

Recently, I was having lunch with two college presidents. We were whining about this and that when one of them quipped, "When I retire, I'm going to consult for college presidents. And before I set foot on any campus, I will have already written, 'After careful analysis I have concluded that you need to communicate more with the board and with your employees.' Trustees and faculty will hail my insight, and everyone will be dazzled by my speed." He can't miss.

For a while I thought the information age might satisfy our appetite for communication. I thought wrong. Technology is creating exponential advances in communication. I have two graduate degrees in communication, but I'm still not sure that I understand the revolution that is taking place. Effective communication may be the most basic requirement of the twenty-first century leader. These days, the leader who claims, "I tried everything to reach you but we couldn't seem to connect" is going to get caught lying. With current tools, anyone can communicate, and any channel that involves electricity will leave a trail. Modern technology blows up all of our excuses for failing to communicate with those we lead.

One of the most important steps leaders can take in becoming better communicators begins with the recognition that the phrase,

"What we have here is a failure to communicate," made famous in *Cool Hand Luke*, is always wrong What leaders have is not a failure to communicate but a failure to communicate effectively.

I try to operate on the assumption that we never fail to communicate; we just fail to communicate the messages we intend. Even silence can be taken as a message. It all depends on our audience. Our audience makes the final call on what our communication, or lack thereof, means. So not only was the utterance in *Cool Hand Luke* wrong, Humpty Dumpty and Alice didn't get it right either:

> "I don't know what you mean by 'glory,'" Alice said.
>
> Humpty Dumpty smiled contemptuously. "Of course you don't—till I tell you. I meant 'there's a nice knock-down argument for you!'"
>
> "But 'glory' doesn't mean 'a nice knock-down argument,'" Alice objected.
>
> "When I use a word," Humpty Dumpty said, in rather a scornful tone, "it means just what I choose it to mean—neither more nor less.'"

Wouldn't it be nice if Humpty were right? I made a light-hearted remark to a friend and witnessed an epic meltdown. When I explained what I meant, he didn't buy it. I told the truth, but what I meant didn't matter. We need to view the receivers of our messages as sovereign. We want to think words have some universal meaning that everyone gets. They don't. Ultimately, people's filters and perceptions present them with advice on which of our messages they will receive and how they will interpret them. Our job is to wrap our messages in clarity. Effective communication is a match between the message intended and the message heard.

I used to write subtle and respectful, non-pushy gift appeals. Actually, I still do, but three years into being a college president I got smacked with the awareness that my letters were communicating the wrong message to some people. A man said to me, "I don't even open my mail from you anymore. The only time I ever hear from you is when you want my money." So, in February 1990, I started writing monthly newsletters to alumni, friends, and parents of our students. I throw all kinds of news into these Kiplinger-type letters, but I never say too much about our financial needs. I've received far more thank-you notes for these twenty-five-hundred-word notes than for anything else I've done in my professional life. The information represents just one of the messages people receive when they get the newsletter. I'm also communicating values, priorities, and that we care enough about our friends to keep them informed. I've learned that when I get done writing one of these informal, and occasionally irreverent, letters I'd better edit it for between-the-lines messages. I've been scolded for what I didn't say, and for what that communicated. I've learned a great deal about communication from this monthly discipline.

The twenty-first century leader faces formidable communication interference and competition. Skill and persistence in communicating effectively will correlate directly with a leader's success. Leaders will have to think not only about message sending, but they will need to study the communication environments in which messages are flying back and forth. The message constitutes only one part of the communication process. Last night I sent an e-mail to my wife of thirty-two years. Her interpretation of what I was trying to say couldn't have been farther from what I intended if we'd never met. Today, we both understand why the craziness she was dealing with last night bent what she heard into something other than the message I was trying to send. In this case, like so many, e-mail was the wrong channel for the message, and I should have known that.

The misunderstanding with my wife demonstrates how hearing holds equal status to sending messages in the communication process. Unfortunately, our culture tends to value effective speaking more than it values good listening. Leaders looking to make durable contributions to their groups will always be listening and looking for significant messages. Sometimes we hear about the leader who is a "good communicator, but doesn't listen well." There is no such animal. The good leader who doesn't listen resembles the good driver who frequently ends up at the wrong place. Leaders who communicate well listen, probe, read, study, and respect their various audiences. Communication is not simply the act of sending messages.

THE TOP SIX LISTENING CONCLUSIONS

The best way for us to learn is to ask questions—but we need to listen to more than just the answers to our questions. We need to be in a listening frame of mind. I have a friend who does something amazing. When you speak to him, he closes his mouth, looks you in the eye, doesn't interrupt, asks you a question or two to make sure he understands, and, as near as I can tell, cares about what you say to him. I find this behavior startling but impressive. He's definitely a collector's item—someone who listens and learns. Because I want to be more like my friend, I've thought a lot about listening. Here are my top six conclusions about listening:

People like to be heard. There is a gap between what I have learned about listening and how well I do it; when it comes to listening, people give you more points for doing it than for understanding it.

We should listen twice as much as we speak. There's a reason God gave us two ears and one mouth. Do the math.

We are socially conditioned to not listen. In an age of extraordinary information overload, tuning out has become a basic means of survival. Interference has become so relentless that it is very difficult to discriminate between the message and the noise.

Listening is more of an attitude than a skill. I discovered this principle when I was in prison—visiting. I was giving a seminar in 1980 at the Anamosa State Penitentiary in rural Iowa. It was a level-IV prison primarily for violent offenders. As I was about to walk into a room, I glanced down at the prisoner sign-in sheet. What I saw stopped me in my tracks. More than seventy-five prisoners had signed in with only six-digit numbers—no sign of a name. When I walked to the front of the room and looked at rows of desperate faces, I decided if I didn't do anything else that weekend, I would learn and use every prisoner's name. I couldn't wait to hear each man announce the name that had been taken away from him, and to my amazement, those names stuck like glue in my mind. In reflecting on this experience, I realized that when I really care, I really listen.

The best measures of the attitude behind your listening are the frequency and depth of your inquisitiveness. If, in our efforts to become better listeners, we don't start with our attitudes toward whomever or whatever we need to hear, we will simply become better imposters. We would be more honest to simply say, "Good afternoon, I have become quite skilled at faking interest in what you have to say." Or, "Good afternoon, I'm about to listen only to your ideas which will reinforce what I have already decided." Or, "Good afternoon, I am about to pay the price of listening to you briefly in order that I might inform you, not so briefly." Ambrose Bierce, in *The Devil's Dictionary,* defines heaven as "a place where the wicked cease from troubling you with talk of their personal affairs, and the good listen with attention while you expound your own." Check yourself. Do you question? Do you probe? Do you dig? Do you care?

Listening requires preparation. We should be as thoughtful about preparing to listen as we are about preparing a speech. Good listening requires preparation, concentration, and reflection. Get ready to hear, focus on your source, and then review what you heard. I've discovered that remembering the names of folks I meet will never happen if I'm not ready to hear the name in the first place. I don't give myself a chance to forget.

THE LISTENER'S TOOLBOX

The following are my communication axioms for twenty-first century leaders. Whoever follows these rules can provide leadership, whether in a position of authority or not:

"Sending" is not a smart way for leaders to think about communication. Communication is a transaction, not an action. Leaders need to consider the simultaneous interaction of themselves, their messages, the channels they use, and their intended receivers when they communicate.

When it comes to initiating communication, too often is a better mistake than too infrequently. Most leaders do not communicate with group members as often as they think they do. Initiating the communication process invites feedback while providing group members with awareness and understanding.

You are a poor judge of your listening skills. We need to seek feedback from those we lead in order to determine the extent to which they feel heard by us. Supervisors should include two-way communication effectiveness as a part of their performance reviews.

It's better to be insultingly clear than respectfully unclear. Don't be afraid of spelling things out. One of the biggest communication obstacles for leaders is that they know what they mean; hence, their ability to judge their clarity is compromised.

Words are overrated. We expect too much from words. A word is simply an abstract symbol until a human being attaches some meaning. We get into trouble when we think words possess universal meaning; what "no" means to me is not what "no" means to a five year old. Assume words are clues to what we mean—give as many clues as necessary.

Questions are underrated. Leaders need to be listeners, and the best listeners are always skilled questioners. They've come to terms with the shortcomings of words and with the way their own filters can tweak a message. They don't assume they have grasped your meaning, so they probe and clarify. These are the people we love to be around, because they seem to care about understanding our favorite topic—ourselves.

Inferences are risky. When my brother was a junior in high school, he went through the terrifying experience of being served liver while dining at a friend's house. In an enormous act of courage, he fought off gag reflexes and choked down the slimy organ in a couple of painful swallows. Dear Mrs. Carmean, mistaking politeness for enjoyment, insisted he have the last piece. His protests were futile; she could just tell that he really liked liver. Asking and believing always serve us better than assuming we understand.

Effective communication is powerful. Somehow, imperfect messengers using imprecise terms and facing our perceptual fortresses still manage to communicate with the power to inspire or devastate us. When we do communicate effectively, the results justify almost any amount of effort required.

Empathizing improves responding. One of the primary ways that I've defined my own maturity is by periodically measuring the amount of time it takes a thought entering my head to come barging out of my mouth. Thinking about how the person with whom we're communicating will hear our next expression can transform our message-sending effectiveness.

Thinking the best is the best kind of thinking. There's a lot of guesswork involved in communication. When we don't have all the information about a situation or why someone acted in a certain way, we fill in the blanks with our guesses. We can't help it. Nature abhors a vacuum; so does human nature. When we think the best with our guesses, we convey trust and optimism. When we make uncharitable assumptions about others, we convey mistrust and cynicism. Which leader would you want to follow?

GIVING FEEDBACK

C.K. Chesterton once said, "If something's worth doing, it's worth doing badly." I think he was referring to various confessions of the soul. If you need to say you're sorry, it's better to stumble through a poorly expressed apology than remain silent because you don't know what to say. Chesterton's aphorism applies to many communication opportunities. Feedback, even ineptly expressed performance feedback, if respectful, is better than no feedback at all. We simply can't make smart adjustments in our efforts if we don't have feedback mechanisms. Organizations with a "cybernetic culture" (one in which feedback helps us chart our course as we go) stay nimble and adaptive.

I served as youth pastor for a magnificent Presbyterian church in downtown Pittsburgh during my doctoral studies. One Sunday, after I'd been greeting folks as they scrambled out of the sanctuary (churches welcome people to enter, then make them stand in line to leave), the senior pastor told me I wasn't focusing during my perfunctory "God bless you; don't let the door hit you on the way out" routine. In fact, he claimed I was looking down the line to see if anyone interesting had picked my less-crowded door. I learned later that my brother-in-law had been his informant. I could not have known at the time that no small part of my living would be made pumping hands, but to this day, every time my duties call on me to greet folks individually, I hear echoes of that very helpful feedback.

Chesterton was right. Feedback is so important that any direct, well-intentioned expression probably helps. But direct feedback is not an easy skill to develop. There are, however, a few basic feedback instincts that we can adopt:

Mixing the peas with the mashed potatoes. I've found that holding *corrective* feedback until I have *affirming* feedback can take the bad taste

55

out of sessions in which I'm asking for changes. Timing is everything. Held too long, negative feedback is difficult for the hearer to put into context, and it loses the impact of immediacy. Instant correction, however, feels like nagging. If we try to soften the instantaneous correction with some kind of gold star that we quickly think up, we can send a mixed message that causes them to bobble the main point. I think that regularly scheduled meetings are the ideal time to provide accumulated feedback, both affirming and corrective. Frankly, I'm not as good as I sound on this and I need to improve.

Assuming good intentions. As a young academic dean, I had to tell a faculty member that her coworkers found her very defensive. How do you deliver that message? If she defended herself, it proved my point. If she agreed, it proved my point. She couldn't win. So, in trying to think of some nice way to rebuild her self-system, which I feared I might dismantle, I stumbled upon her heart. This woman was the most loyal faculty member in our division, and she fired both barrels on anyone who criticized us or her efforts to make us better. So I sat down with this woman in a different frame of mind than one of simply going about the task of explaining how distasteful people found her defective character. I assumed her defensiveness was out of loyalty rather than weakness. I assumed that she wanted to grow, which in fact she did. She acknowledged that considering questions and criticisms as threats, rather than as ways to improve, had impeded her development. She wasn't happy, but at least she didn't strike me.

Thinking of feedback as a map. Our employees and our organizations must know when they're headed in the right direction and when they deviate—and so must we. The leaders who hold a deep value for feedback will create cybernetic climates that can keep our organizations on course.

LEADING FROM THE MIDDLE

In the twenty-first century, I do not expect we will often hear the description of someone as a "strong leader but weak communicator." To be sure, we will encounter leaders with limited skills in public speaking or writing or even in interpersonal communication. But all effective leaders will have at least one communication tool in their kits with which they can proclaim their dreams and visions with penetrating power. Messages communicated weakly will never be heard amidst the sheer volume of information rushing through the ever-expanding channels of communication.

We find ourselves in a new age. Information and learning have taken over organizational cultures once dominated by mining and manufacturing. The power of leaders has been distributed throughout more federated groups and organizations. People weave cocoons to protect themselves from information bombardments. Everything about contemporary society raises the stakes for leaders to communicate effectively. I wonder how many of the people I lead find themselves in turbulent situations and desperately need me to communicate with them. Some people characterize me as a good communicator, but no matter how skilled I might be, I'm not a good communicator if my silence sends out messages of negligence. If we wish to lead people, we must manage messages and manage them well.

Almost all of the current communication textbooks present the evolution of communication theory as moving from an action model (message sent one direction), to an interaction model (messages sent back and forth), and then to a transaction model (messages exchanged simultaneously). To me, these three models represent rungs of communication quality. Not long ago, I sent a message by e-mail to our students (action model). I received a note back from a student named Amber saying she would like to meet with me; so I sent her a note back (interaction model) urging her to stop me the next time she saw me. The next day Amber approached me in the Union Building and introduced herself. Our short conversation was very pleasant for both of us (transactional model). The potential for transactional communication rises sharply when leaders are visible and accessible. Not only does being in the middle increase the frequency of direct communication transactions, it puts us in a better position to manage the meaning of our messages when our schedules force us to use the action approach. Only *Wizard of Oz* leaders can stay behind the curtain, and as we know, that doesn't work forever.

Chapter Six

Virtuous Leadership

In December 1991, through a series of bizarre circumstances, I tracked down NBA basketball player Steve Alford and hired him as coach for Manchester College's 0-6 men's basketball team. At the time, he'd just been cut from a West Coast team and was in conversation with the Boston Celtics. I'd read that he wanted to be a college coach and did not like the NBA very much. So, within thirty-six hours of my first contact we shook hands, and three days later, the most beloved basketball figure in America's most storied basketball state had moved with his wonderful (and pregnant) wife, Tanya, to North Manchester, Indiana.

After watching Steve for one week of practice, I concluded that he would become a very good college coach. After watching him for a month, I thought he might also become a very good leader. Then on Monday, May 18, 1992, I thought, "This guy might become a *great* leader."

It was the morning after the Alfords got home from the hospital with their newborn child. I dashed over to their house to meet baby Kory. Everything was typical new parents-new baby stuff until the new dad and I walked out to my car. In a soft rain, Steve said, "I want to thank you."

Although his words were a bit halting, I thought he was thanking me for stopping by. "Are you kidding?" I replied. "I wanted to see Kory."

Then he said, "I'm not talking about that. I want to thank you that I'm here. If I had signed with the Celtics, I might have been in Cleveland (where the Celtics were playing the Cavaliers in the NBA playoffs) and missed seeing my son being born. Can you imagine how horrible that would have been?"

What I could scarcely imagine was that this twenty-seven-year-old, who dreamed every day of his Hoosier childhood of playing in the NBA, felt that seeing the birth of his son was much more important than being a professional basketball player. It was then that I knew he really meant what he said about his values.

When a leader's virtue rebuffs culture's most seductive invitations, the power of authenticity is created, and it is a power that can catapult or destroy leadership. Seeing virtue in their leaders gives people the confidence that nothing expedient or self-gratifying can ever divert their leader from doing what is good and right. Sarbanes-Oxley legislation costs U.S. businesses billions of dollars every year, dollars that could go to shareholders, research, charities, or the bottom line. We pay these watchdog dues because of greed, because "leaders" with piles of money sold their integrity to put more on their piles. They did not do what was good and right, and they now live in shame and infamy.

If my list of twenty-first century leadership qualities falls victim to wishful thinking at any point, it is here. I hold the number-two spot in presidential longevity at Whitworth. This endurance should get me at least a couple of pages in the school's next history book. (This recognition inspires me to work hard at kissing up to the university historian.) No doubt my two pages will refer to buildings, money, enrollment, and how weird it was to have a president arrive whose maturity level was indistinguishable from that of the students. But what I want most in those two pages is for someone to remember me as a good person. My target is to be the kind of leader my children imagine me to be. I want to be a leader known for my virtue, as well as for my accomplishments.

I hold a somewhat confused perspective on virtue and ethics, but I hold it tenaciously. I'm even more dogmatic about virtue now than

I was before I got confused. Almost twenty years ago, I got a call from a friend saying he needed to talk to me. Although I loved this guy, I did not necessarily consider him a paragon of Christian virtue. As it turns out, his wife had taken a shine to another guy and wanted out of the marriage. Kids, property, and quite a few years together merely complicated her exit; she was gone. My job was to support my friend, so we quickly put together a time for golf, eating, and venting.

As we sloshed our way through dinner, passing up few chances to villainize this woman, my buddy confessed his certainty that this was not his wife's first affair. That observation didn't exactly startle me, but his next statement did, and it hurled a wrench into my system of ethics and virtue. Sheepishly, he peeked over his glasses and said, "But I never cheated on her." Incredulously, I asked why.

"Well, I was tempted several times," he said, "but I knew it wasn't right."

Here I was, the lifelong Christian ministering to my secular friend, but I knew that if I were in his shoes, only my reverence and fear of God would have delivered me from the suspicion and vengeance that would have provided the perfect excuse for adultery. I realized that I had never constructed a personal morality independent of faith.

Several years after this incident, I got hit with the second major assault on my belief that virtue came only from obedience to God. After I'd spent almost a year consulting for Phil Clement, the president of DeVry, Inc., we arranged for a long dinner at which I would give him a summary of my observations. I had found Phil to be a man of towering integrity in everything he did. While sitting on his management team for a year, I never saw Phil budge on his demand for the highest ethical standards in every decision we made. He had become my role model of business virtue. No cracks. Toward the end of our meal together, I had to ask him to reveal the source of all this morality and commitment to his employees.

"My grandfather, I guess," Phil said. "When I was a young boy, he worked for a labor union. He just always told the truth, and he always did what was right. There were no other options. I watched the way he lived."

"But what about honoring and obeying God?" I asked.

"Nah, I'd say it was my grandfather. I've never really given God too much thought," Phil replied.

When I say my commitment to virtue has become stronger now that it's confused, I mean that I no longer hold my original belief in the existential motto of "Eat, drink, and be merry" as the only logical ethic apart from God. I find too many examples of non-faith-based morality for me to accept that there is no good apart from God. I do believe God to be the first source of everything that is good, but a fundamental awareness of what is right and wrong endows all people with certain moral responsibilities. For me personally, ethical resolve still rises from my longing for God's approval, but reinforcing that resolve is a profound awareness of my responsibility as a citizen of the human community. I believe that for others, not being a person of faith provides no excuse for moral compromise.

Leaders claiming all this stuff should be left to philosophers and graduate students are dangerous. They duck their moral responsibilities, hiding behind the question of "Whose morality gets to be in charge?" That's not a bad question, but it's a bad shield. We should have no tolerance for people in positions of leadership with cavalier attitudes toward virtue, no matter what excuses they hide behind.

Virtue in our leaders is more important now than ever. When organizations were such that leaders and members worked in more circumscribed roles, moral detours were a little easier to spot. Now that our line of sight isn't so straight, trust must replace surveillance. Leaders must rise to repair the moral disintegration making our society outrageous and absurd. Unless we discover some kind of moral fluoridation that prevents ethical cavities, our leaders must serve as our moral exemplars and physicians. I believe the twenty-first century citizen will demand leaders whose competence *and* virtue can be trusted.

Contributing to the challenge of providing virtuous leadership is the enormous pressure leaders feel to produce results. Leaders of publicly held companies live and die on quarterly earnings. Even not-for-profit organizations can ill afford to make a good long-term decision if it throws the annual operating budget into the red. Red ink means red flags for donors who want to invest in a winner. I know that the intense pressure I place on myself can divert my attention from moral considerations. I commit sins of omission more than of commission, but that's not much to be proud of. Leaders need to recognize that virtue is good business. It delivers good long-term results because it inspires trust and loyalty in those we lead.

The tall influence of James McGregor Burns both helps and hurts the case for leaders' virtue. When he writes, "Leadership occurs when one or more persons engage with others in such a way that leaders and followers raise one another to higher levels of motivation and morality" (1978, 4), he helps make the virtue point. But when he excludes from his definition of leaders people who use their power nefariously, he lulls us into danger.

By Burns's definition, Bill Clinton was not a leader because he failed to raise people to higher levels of morality. I think Bill Clinton was a very strong leader—disgusting in his personal morality but certainly a leader, sometimes good and sometimes bad. By defining "leaders" as necessarily morally uplifting, we weaken our position to *demand* their virtue. I agree with Barbara Kellerman (ironically, of the James McGregor Burns Academy of Leadership at the University of Maryland) who objects to Burns's odd, albeit influential, definition of leadership:

> One problem with what is arguably a redefinition of the word "leadership" is that it separates those who are in the field from those who are outside it. Although most scholars and practitioners who are in any way associated with Leadership Studies... assume that to lead is to do right, those outside this still narrow band make no such assumption. Most folks use the word leader as it has always been used: to refer to those able to draw on sources of power, authority and influence to get others to fall into line. In ordinary conversations, for example, Slobodan Milosevic is referred to as the leader of the Serbs, no matter what he does ... While outside the rarified halls of academe I have yet to hear anyone call Milosevic a (Burns's term) "power wielder," I know full well that for most of us in leadership studies, the term leader simply does not apply. (2000, 69)

I think Kellerman's deliverance from the jargon of Burns and other academics better positions the average person to demand virtue from those who wish to lead.

What can the twenty-first century leader do to become more virtuous? I have three suggestions that have worked well for me:

1. *Identify the virtues that you want to define your leadership.* Trying to move in the general direction of being virtuous won't work. If you achieve anything, it will probably be little more than a feeling of self-righteousness, which is definitely not a virtue. Ask the folks you lead which virtues they most want in their leader. Read other people's lists to stimulate your thinking. Recently, I received a list in the mail from Gordon B. Hinckley, president of The Church of Jesus Christ of Latter-day Saints. He wrote a book onhis top ten virtues:love, honesty, morality, civility, learning, forgiveness and mercy, thrift and industry, gratitude, optimism, and faith (Hinckley 2001). We need to increase the frequency of our discourse on ethics and morality.

I remember a great discussion our family had on virtues. We were on a road trip from Washington to Chicago when my wife whipped out a tape of Bill Bennett's *Book of Virtues* and made the kids and me listen. Because I was still mad at Bennett for trying to kill the whole Department of Education when he served as its head, I supported the kids' demands that we break from virtue for a few tunes now and then. On one of those breaks, we happened to beam up the O.J. Simpson chase on our car radio. Somehow, the irony of virtue and O.J. coming out of the stereo in sequence stirred deep and important questions in our children. We had a great conversation about what is right. (By the way, I decided Bennett couldn't be all bad when I found out he once went on a date with Janis Joplin.) Think specifically about the virtues you want your people to be able to count on from you.

2. *Commit yourself to openness.* Life is filled with temptations that intensify when nobody's looking. Sometimes I have been tempted to live a bit more luxuriously on my business expense account than I would on my own money, a practice I find lacking in virtue. So I've told faculty members that they are welcome to review my expense reports if they have concerns. Sometimes, especially when I travel, I'm tempted to look at garbage on the Internet, a practice I find lacking in virtue.

So I've given permission to our information technology people to look at my site-visit logs.

At times we're all tempted to conceal information that we feel others can't handle or will misunderstand. That feels pretty paternalistic. Certainly we deal with confidential information that should not be disclosed, but what are we saying about our coworkers when we hide information only because "they can't handle it?" Or maybe we conceal information because it's not really any of their business—yet we want them to own their work and support our mission. Our business *is* their business. I don't consider openness to be some kind of desperate measure to save us from ourselves; it just keeps the light on. Virtue always stands up under scrutiny. There is a certain honesty belonging to those who live their lives in the light, and honesty is definitely a virtue.

3. Be honest with yourself. In Erving Goffman's *The Presentation of Self in Everyday Life* (1959), he argues that we all have three selves: the public self, the private self, and the ideal self. I think that many times we're not honest with these three selves. We pretend to be someone we're not (the public self), we long to be someone we're not (the ideal self), and we convince ourselves we're someone we're not (the private self). Leaders easily fall prey to personal dishonesty. Too many people blow compliments in their ears. A self-system with reasonable consistency among the three selves breeds higher levels of integrity than one in which we present a very different self than the one we keep private.

The most important moment in my own efforts to become more virtuous occurred over a yearlong period in which I came to grips with my hidden but abundant selfishness. Faced with two situations in which my public image would get battered no matter what I decided, I asked, "What would the real Bill Robinson do?" My shameful but honest answer was that he would do what would be best for his public self. I discovered I'd been so impressed with my public self that I didn't notice the rot in my private self. I had boxes of clippings that proved I was a good guy. I had seldom looked within, and when I did, I chose carefully what I wanted to see. I was long on God-talk but short on spirituality. Only when my selfishness caved in on me was I driven inward in any kind of honest way. I had dipped to the point where virtue, ironically, came within reach. It was worth the crash.

LEADING FROM THE MIDDLE

I've tossed around terms such as "virtue," "morality," "integrity," and "ethics" without strictly defining them, as though they were interchangeable. There are certain differences among these terms, but leaders know what they mean, and they know how badly leadership needs to stand on virtue and moral courage. Our society cries out for moral leadership. Our leaders must come through as good human beings.

There is something about being among those we lead that calls forth our virtue. At close range, we are exposed. Being in the middle serves as both the cause and effect of our leadership strength. When we are in their midst, people can see most clearly whether we possess the goodness to deserve their confidence. It is where they can discover if we are the same person up close as we are up front.

The end of Psalm 78 offers a beautiful statement of an ordinary person of integrity providing extraordinary leadership: "God chose David and took him from the sheep pens; from tending the sheep, he brought him to being the shepherd of his people … And David shepherded them with integrity, and with skillful hands he led them."

CHAPTER SEVEN

DRIVEN AND RHYTHMIC LEADERSHIP

Leading is hard work—a lot harder than just being in charge. Good leaders love the hunt. The more pressure the better. Their favorite substance in the entire world is adrenaline. They'll stand on their heads to help people achieve the group's goal. They claim they have higher standards for themselves than for those they lead, and they're lying—they have high standards for all living creatures. They're always pushing themselves. They're calm in the whirlpools and they're whirlpools in the calm, but they're seldom resting. They feed on getting the job done.

In the twenty-first century, leading is still hard work and leaders still have to push themselves, but it would be a mistake for leaders to push as they have in the past. Earlier, I discussed the mounting pressure created by a results-oriented culture. Leaders feel it intensely. But this unforgiving results orientation can also be used by leaders for replenishment. Because getting the job done is more important than being the one who logs the most hours at work, we can take control of our schedules in ways that exploit our personal and professional peaks.

Over the years, I have come to accept rhythm as one of the most powerful life forces. Nature is unhaltingly rhythmic. Nothing can stop the march of seasons, tides, birth cycles, and the Chicago Cubs' September swoons. In everyday life we can attempt to harness or create rhythm, but it's hard to fight the flow. The twenty-first century's exaltation of results, whether idolatrous or pragmatic, provides leaders an opportunity to drive and renew themselves in concert with the rhythms of life and work. I'm not sure the current judge of results ever intended to be lenient about how and when leaders push themselves, but the judge has no choice. The punch-clock of inputs got unplugged when the law of outputs was put in force. In other words, leaders can now take the liberty to do what works best, rather than what's conventional.

The most important way leaders can take advantage of this opportunity is to work in rhythm with their personal and organizational productivity cycles. The best way for us to keep driving without burning ourselves out is to show up at the right times in the right places. Patterns and cycles create tides, and therefore opportunities, in virtually all types of work.

In my job, I've found predictable moments when my involvement has exponential impact. For example, I've noticed the first ten days of November seem to crush the spirits of students on a semester calendar. They've been at school a long time without a break, and Thanksgiving vacation still feels distant. They're tired from midterms, and the darkness that ran off Daylight Savings Time announces winter's imminence. These are the days when I try to eat in the dining hall, send e-mails, have students over to the house, etc. On the other hand, in the fourth week of September, student life is so good they don't know I exist. It is not a time when I'll get much bang for the spend-time-with-students buck. All groups, organizations, and leaders have cycles that need to be monitored. Misreads and absences can result in problems that could be avoided.

Knowing when to show up is no more important than knowing when not to show up. This is where most leaders lose control of their drive. Too often, our involvement and presence act as an oil spill, wasting our fuel and making a mess of the situational ecology. But our tankers don't start and stop easily. We're directed, we have momentum, and we can navigate the shallow waters when we get to them. We go to everything. We're omnipresent. This is where dumb and dangerous support each other. Leaders must drive themselves hard, but they need to be smart about it. Exhaustible fuel supplies need time to replenish. Excessive involvement diminishes leader impact or creates unhealthy dependency.

In addition to reading the rhythms of the organizations we lead, we need to understand our own cycles. Chuck Boppell, past CEO of Sizzler Restaurants (and past chair of the Whitworth University board of trustees), is a great leader. Everybody in the food industry respects him. As a turnaround specialist committed to fairness and compassion, he's the consummate paradoxical leader, a shrewd and uncompromising analyst with a gentle touch. Chuck's personal cycles are very interesting. It would be fair to say that he shifts gears very deliberately, which is why the food companies he's been hired to run (Taco Bell, Pizza Hut, La Salsa, etc.) get turned around very quickly. Knowing himself, Chuck works in large blocks. He drives relentlessly, and then takes a pretty big chunk of time between jobs or between cycles within a job, to recover. Chuck's style would not work for most mortals. When he's in his work zone, nobody comes close to his productivity. (Actually, he will slam on the brakes when his wife says "Stop!" or when one of his grandchildren flashes a smile at him.) When he relaxes, he's awfully good at being a million miles from work.

Chuck Boppell's style shows how the secret of replenishment for driven leaders lies in understanding their personal and organizational rhythms. In the past ten years, I've initiated hardly any lunch meetings— I've attended a quite a few, but I never set them up unless I'm traveling. When I'm in town, lunch is best spent for me working or working out. I eat less, I spend less, I travel less, and I enjoy myself more when I don't go out for lunch. On the other hand, mid-morning coffee meetings work great for me. Because I usually do deskwork in my office at home from five thirty to nine thirty AM, mid-morning conversations and caffeine provide a great launch into my office workday. Having observed these patterns, my assistant arranges my activities in synchrony with the rhythms of my life and job.

There is one other type of rhythm that leaders must exploit. It is the mystical rhythm of success. My wife, Bonnie, is a professional pianist/organist with an uncommon gift of musicality. She grabs the emotions of her listeners, bathes them with beauty and meaning, and then returns a little more than she took. For her, rhythm is everything, but not just the rhythm of meter and beat. She also waits longingly for the rare, unexplainable rhythm that presents flow and ease to artists, athletes, carpenters, speakers, writers, and all who perform rhythmic tasks. I can sit in the audience and tell when this phantom guest is paying Bonnie a visit. She knows that I know. A beautiful legato unites the notes that flow through her. She has become a messenger of something exquisite. Athletes call this "being in the zone." What is hard technically becomes easy.

This blessing is neither "the zone" nor an out-of- body experience; it is being in rhythm with our task. Frankly, no one knows exactly how to get this genie out of the bottle. How many times have we seen the replay of Michael Jordan looking to the bench after draining another three-pointer and shrugging his shoulders? Not even the best basketball player in the solar system knew why he'd gotten so hot. But leaders must search diligently for every condition that brings them as close as possible to this rhythm. When we have it, in whatever area of our leadership, we need to exploit it. I give an average of three or four speeches per week. I would have to say it's a strength. Occasionally, a special oratorical rhythm will show up for weeks at a time. And then it's gone. I'm back to normal

Driven leaders crave efficiency and effectiveness. Both their productivity and their durability depend on doing the right things well. I have become convinced that driven leaders who ignore or fight the rhythms of their lives and jobs are the leaders who crash and burn. Success and longevity are the rewards for those in concert with the natural forces of the very hard work of providing leadership.

LEADING FROM THE MIDDLE

I find replenishment and perspective when I'm close to the core of our mission. Time spent with the students and staff generally knocks me back on course. One summer, my board chair wanted me to shake hands on six more years at Whitworth. I had just completed my fifteenth year as a college president. In addition to working on my day job, the year was one in which I served as chair of the Spokane Regional Chamber of Commerce board of trustees and cochaired with our newly elected mayor a huge effort designed to reduce regional poverty. Going into the year, I had pretty much hoped the university would run on autopilot. It didn't. So the thought of six more years, after one in which I ran myself into the ground, depressed me.

I knew if I were to take this on, which is what my family wanted, I would have to get back into the natural rhythm and flow of my work. I had been doing too much stopping and starting as I shifted from duty to duty. The strategy I settled on for getting back in the groove was to get back in the middle. I didn't need to reinvent my job; I needed to reintroduce myself to it. So, I took a semester and virtually canceled my travel. I taught a class, met with every department on campus, spent more time in the residence halls, and got myself back involved in the direct delivery of Whitworth's heart-and-mind education. It was restoration by immersion, and it turned out great.

I'm convinced that leaders who spend all of their time out in front of their people lose perspective and stumble into inefficient patterns. More often than not, their throttle remains wide open, but they waste energy. Getting back into the middle of the people and mission gets them back into the currents that best carry their considerable drive. They are renewed by the mission they are called to lead.

REFLECTION
Enough Is Enough

Perhaps the most liberating mindset I've developed over the years is a pretty well-formed concept of "enough." I make enough money. I get enough recognition. And because of that, I am free from making career decisions to get me more of either. Further, my colleagues are free from goals that are more about pride than about good sense. I don't feel as though I'm living the life of Sisyphus—daily pushing the rock up the hill. Now, let me be quick to say that my ability to flip the "enough" switch hardly lightens the driving ambition that wrecks my sleep on many nights. I still worry about little things because I'm too dumb to notice worry doesn't help. Unfortunately, my recognition and acceptance of "enough" is restricted to big stuff. But in those areas where I have freed myself from the more, more syndrome, I have been blessed with a contentment that no amount of money or recognition can bring.

SECTION SUMMARY

I'm not all that sappy, but once in a while the smallest thing will just overwhelm me. On my first day back to campus after a two-month sabbatical in which I wrote much of what is contained in this book, I decided to go on a thirty-minute run through campus. I'm not much for exercise that doesn't involve a ball or an enemy, but I enjoy lumbering around our grounds during the summer and fall. Brilliant mums and marigolds glow in the lush green grass on what has to be the most beautiful campus in the northwestern America. As I was looking over the summer's capital construction projects, I noticed that our early return football, soccer, and volleyball athletes were beating the heat with early morning practices. I couldn't stay away from them. Through grins, waves, hollers, and even being thrown a pass (which my memory now has me catching without breaking stride), I began to feel this enormous sense of privilege.

I had spent all summer thinking about leading, reminding myself that with the best leaders, it's never about the leader. On that run I felt a warm purity that rose out of a deep belief that I do what I do for them. Maybe it was just oxygen deprivation, but it sure felt good. I decided to wander through the dining hall during their lunch break. I walked out of there assured that I am called to eat lunch with students.

Sometimes I wonder if God made me for the singular purpose of hanging around with collegians. I don't know, but here's what I do know beyond any doubt: our students have made me a better leader than I was ever meant to be. I can supply certifiable proof that I have just what it takes to be utterly ineffective. But these young people have placed before me the text of their needs and hopes that is both readable and inspiring. Accepting their invitations for me to lead them has given me worth, direction, and honor. In that sense, they have led my growth. Without words, they asked me for a standard of leadership that felt well beyond my ability to provide. Without trying, they made me do my best.

I have suggested that the twenty-first century will call forth leadership that is paradoxical, secure, communicative, inspiring, virtuous, and driven. All of these qualities work better at close range than from a pedestal. We must be touched by the needs and longings of those who would follow us, and ours must touch them. We must lead from the middle of our people—the very people who have entrusted us with their confidence.

SECTION II

TWENTIETH CENTURY
APPROACHES TO LEADERSHIP

The twentieth century was a period of great centrifugal force, both in organizations and in the ways in which they were led. Tall, top-heavy organizations flattened under the gravitational pull of customers whose needs were met on the ground, not on the top floors of corporate headquarters. As these organizations localized into branch operations, profit centers, and other region-based outposts, leadership also spun away from the center. Managers in the field worked off goals and objectives rather than procedures and policy manuals. To be successful, they needed the kind of authority that would empower them to achieve outcomes rather than simply enforce company rules.

As this organizational responsibility marched away from the center, leadership had to go with it. Corporate kings managing the field by remote control could never be as effective as regional leaders who understood customer demands and local cultures. This centrifugal spread prompted leadership theorists to consider the growing evidence that leadership did not always flow from the DNA of those at the top.

This section highlights the movement of leadership thinking in the twentieth century. Like organizational structure, approaches to leadership moved away from the center. In the early 1900s, leaders were thought of as the fortunate few who bore the deeply embedded traits of the folks in charge. In the middle of the century, leadership *styles* replaced the emphasis on *traits*. Although most leaders found some approaches more natural than others, styles could be learned and developed in ways that a person's most basic traits could not. But, unfortunately, no single style always worked well. So, the next question asked if different situations called for different styles. Finally, by the end of the twentieth century, leadership thinking had moved from traits to styles to a focus on leadership behaviors that were bred by the organizational culture. When this final wave hit the beach, everybody in the organization got splashed. No one was excluded from the opportunity or even the responsibility to provide leadership. I heard about one corporate executive who told her people, "When you're dealing with the customer, you become the CEO." I don't know if the story is true, but it captures the spirit of decentralized leadership.

It is tempting to see these different approaches as corrections of their flawed predecessors. I am convinced, however, that wisdom can be found in all three of these leadership schools. This section attempts to mine that wisdom.

CHAPTER EIGHT

TRAIT-BASED LEADERSHIP

In the summer of 1969, I worked in a factory cutting steel. Evidently, I'd botched one of the machinist's orders, or at least that's what I assumed while he was screaming at me. After he stormed off, leaving me teary-eyed, another machinist who had witnessed the event came over and told me I had no reason to be upset. "He's Polish," my comforter explained in a heavy German brogue. "He can't help it. People are like dogs. Germans are like collies; Poles are like mongrels. They're born that way." I didn't find much comfort in his racism, but it did become clear to me that his generation and culture felt that "born that way" was a more powerful influence on behavior than socialization.

In the early years after scholars placed the suffix "-ship" on the backside of "leader," "leadership" referred to the traits of a leader, and "born that way" described how most folks thought about being a leader. This tight connection between "leader" and "leadership" was reinforced by a particular research methodology and a huge, extraordinarily well-organized laboratory. The laboratory was the United States Armed Forces, perfectly arranged by rank.

In its simplest form, this correlational research method would identify or determine the position or rank of subjects, then look at how they scored on measures such as talkativeness, humor, physical appearance, originality, etc. If, for example, fifty lieutenants scored significantly higher on a creativity test than fifty privates, creativity was declared a leadership trait. Hence, the variables with the most direct correlation to an advanced rank were considered leadership traits. If a study shows, for example, that there is a "significantly positive" correlation between height and annual income, we can only conclude that the taller a person is, the more money he or she is likely to make. However, we can't say from the research that height improves earning power (or that being rich makes you taller).

Because of these limits in the research methods, the traits found among leaders in these early studies are not necessarily the *cause* of their leadership. They are simply the characteristics that people associated with leaders. In fact, the overwhelming conclusion of today's leadership scholars is that "the early studies failed to support the basic premise of the trait approach that a person must possess a particular set of traits to become a successful leader. Although some traits appeared widely relevant for different kinds of leaders, these traits were neither necessary nor sufficient to ensure leadership success" (Yukl 2005, 255).

As with most research efforts, the leadership characteristics found from study to study varied. It almost seems as though the principal criterion for choosing leadership subjects was their availability. However, a broad sweep of the findings suggests that the most frequently found characteristics in leaders included three traits related to effort and four traits related to personality:

Traits related to effort:

- Desire to excel

- Aggressiveness

- Energy

Traits related to personality:

- Originality

- Popularity

- Humor

- Sociability

While these qualities continue to facilitate leadership (although their individual favor has waxed and waned through the years), it's interesting to note what's missing. Neither intelligence nor physical characteristics correlated as highly with being a leader as the above traits. Apparently, back then a person could attain a leadership position without having the native intelligence that our information age now exalts. (Actually, in eighteen of twenty-three studies reviewed by Bass and Stogdill, the average leader did test to be more intelligent than the average member of his or her group. However, in five of the studies, too much intelligence proved to hurt the leader's ability to lead the group.)

In academic research, there is always more to be learned about a finding, but there is something to be said for our first impressions. So, I do not dismiss these early studies as anachronistic or culturally outdated. I think some very good ideas came out of our first looks at leadership. Rost also holds this point of view, citing four major studies conducted in the 1980s that he argues were, in essence, dressed-up versions of trait theory (1991, 28).

In the post-traits periods, it will become clear that the qualities listed above are neither necessary in their entirety nor sufficient individually to constitute good leadership. Nevertheless, the presence of these characteristics can be very helpful in supporting effective leadership.

TRAITS RELATED TO EFFORT

I was once the guest of a U. S. Congressman at a dinner on a 147-foot yacht. The owner of the boat was hosting the transportation committee of the United States House of Representatives. Not only did this nice man own the boat, he also owned a trucking company and rather hoped that this fact would not get lost on the fifteen congressional delegates who joined him for a little dinner-cruise on the Potomac.

Somehow over the course of the evening I had a chance to ask our host how he'd built such a successful company. I didn't expect him to make reference to buying off politicians, but I also didn't really expect such a basic answer. Our host simply said, "I love hard work, and I demand it from others."

It's one thing to like hard work, but this guy was foaming at the mouth. His best story was when he encountered some employees standing around at a loading dock with one of his trucks yet to be unloaded. As the story goes, our hard-work advocate ran up to those guys, reached into his pockets, grabbed all his change and flung it at them. He then dipped into his wallet and stated hurling greenbacks at them, all the time screaming, "You thieves, go ahead, take all my money!" Evidently, this man found little difference between laziness and theft.

Traits related to effort carry more of an overtone of virtue than traits related to personality, largely because of their perceived controllability. When I became a college president and saw such learned colleagues leading our rival schools, I thought my only chance of keeping up with these folks would be to outwork them. It was the one thing I could control. Leaders communicate a work ethic more by example than by explanation.

For this reason, it is of no surprise that early studies found three of the most recurring leadership traits were related to effort.

DESIRE TO EXCEL

It was a normal Sunday, the day I set aside all that rages within me to meditate on God's good grace. But that particular Sunday morning a brutish desire to excel rose from my viscera and conquered my brain. I couldn't stop it from coming. This particular defeat of reason started innocently enough. As my wife was leaving to prepare for her duties as church organist, I asked, "Which service are Ben and Bailley (son and daughter) going to?" Bonnie replied that they were not going to church, but were instead participating in a "fun-run" fundraiser at Bailley's high school. For me, "fun run" is an oxymoron, so I should have kept my distance. But when Bailley cooed, "Come on, Dad, run with us; we'll just go easy," I was hooked, as only she can hook me. Although I caved in, I made a solemn covenant with myself that I would jog lazily. I even called one of Ben's friends and made him promise to run with me, just so I wouldn't try to keep up with my rabbit son, knowing he'd break his promise to go easy.

Two minutes before the race, this blood-of-my-blood scoundrel looked at me and said, "Hey dad, you're not capable of going easy," then threw back his head and laughed. He was right; I was already abandoning my vows of moderation. So I spent thirty-nine minutes and twenty-seven seconds torturing myself, running frantically up the side of a mountain because when I stood at the starting line, a voice inside me said, "There's just no way you're taking more than forty minutes to run this sissy course." It was about a week before I could walk without assistance.

The desire to excel can be found in the DNA of every successful leader. The self evidence of this statement is so clear I have chosen not to include rags-to-riches accounts of people who made their ascent using the fuel of this compulsion. Rather, I will focus on the ways in which the drive for excellence needs to be channeled. It's one thing to lose control of that desire and end up with jelly-legs from a stupid decision about a race; it's quite another to be intoxicated by the lure of excellence to the extent that strategic equilibrium and moral sensibilities are lost.

Although much of the research on the connection between the excellence drive and success proved to be positive, some studies have actually found a negative correlation between these two variables. Gary Yukl explains these equivocal findings by suggesting that perhaps the relationship is curvilinear (2005, 270). In other words, we can have too much of a good thing. Up to a certain point, the more drive you have, the more success you get. Beyond that point, your compulsion begins to undermine your success. Yukl suggests that some of the diminishing-return points might be excessive risk or conservatism, unrealistic goals and deadlines, and reluctance to delegate (2005, 270-1). I suppose perfectionism and workaholism also come along as companion viruses of those who let their desire to excel move into the danger zone.

Twenty years ago, at three in the morning in my living room, my dear friend Boyd Wilson, now a brilliant religion professor at Hope College, helped me see my greatest vulnerability related to the excellence drive. Emboldened by too much consumption and too little sleep, I lovingly offered my opinion of his fatal flaw. There must have been a lot of love in the room, because he returned the favor. He said, "Your biggest problem is that you think you have to be better than everybody at everything." After peeling off layers of defensiveness, I began what would be one of my most important professional journeys.

Slowly, painfully, failing and flailing, I became the founder and only member of my own "Winaholics Anonymous." I am still in recovery.

In one statement, my friend pointed out two desire-to-excel problems: breadth and measurement. I was in deep trouble. My breadth problem, "I must be better at everything," was keeping me from delegating. At age thirty-one, I'm sure I thought I was good at everything. Why sacrifice quality in the name of delegation? At the time, I was dean of a fledgling department in a college. I'd been awarded this position because the provost decided to try unleashing my hungry, win-at-all-costs compulsions on this program before deep-sixing it. I did delegation-free administration and taught more than a full-time load. I taught because I felt I was better than the other faculty members, and I didn't charge the college for my teaching because I was obsessed with making our budget. I was going to make this thing work if it killed me, which is what it was in the process of doing. I had lost my balance, and my soul wasn't far behind. But blessed reality came to the rescue. With the help of my friend, I realized that I'm not good at everything. In fact, I'm not good at most things. I never will be. I don't have to be. Whoever said "You can do anything if you really try" was lying. You can't. You might "want to be like Mike," but it isn't going to happen, no matter how many hours you work on your moves. Further, you'll waste a lot of time working on what Mike can do rather than what *you* can do. My effectiveness began to rise when I made peace with the long list of capabilities that God left off my gift list.

The breadth problem had me so busy lunging after excellence in every direction that I probably didn't notice when I stepped onto the treadmill. The term my friend used that cut the deepest, that made me realize I was chasing the unattainable, was "better." I was willing to admit my desire to excel at many things. Virtue can be found in such a desire, but my only measuring device was comparing and competing with others. The poison of "better" is in its relativity. Its achievement depends not only on my progress but also on somebody else's. The fundamental difference between excelling and winning is the difference between an absolute standard and a relative standard. I remember when my high-school daughter's good friend traveled 800 meters in 1:53.87 in the state track meet. Until that day, nobody in the state that year had broken 1:54 in the event. Unfortunately, three guys in the state meet ran faster than 1:53.87, so her friend didn't win, but he did excel.

I hate Vince Lombardi's statement that "Winning isn't everything, it's the only thing"—another great piece of pith from the world of sports. For those of you keeping score at home, when something becomes "everything," it becomes "only." But I do agree that winning is sweet, and can be quite noble if properly understood. Shortly after I became the president of Manchester College in Indiana, we had the 1964 10,000-meter Olympic gold medalist, Billy Mills, come to campus for our lecture series. I vividly remember watching his famous victory, alone in my house, screaming my head off. As we chatted during the afternoon of his arrival, I asked Billy what he was thinking as he mounted that famous, furious kick that gave a couple of Englishmen a good view of his backside crossing the finish line. He told me that every night for two years he went to sleep picturing himself surging at the moment he thought he'd lost the Olympic race. He went on to say that at the final turn of the final lap, he got tangled up and tripped. The moment he stumbled, he thought to himself, "I've lost the race." And at that point he felt the surge. Mills said to me, "Bill, when I felt the surge, I knew I'd won because I reached the goal I'd set for myself. At the time, I didn't really think I'd finish first, but I knew I'd won the race."

It is hard for me to express the liberation I have experienced having redefined "winning the race" in ways that do not depend on the success or failure of others. Our deep desires for excellence must focus on controllable elements. They must be spacious, allowing for coworkers, and even competitors, to excel as well. We share a city with Gonzaga University, our number-three cross-application school in competing for students. Everyone knows how highly I esteem Gonzaga and admire its president, a dear friend. I would bet anything that my public affection for Gonzaga has not cost us one student or one dollar. It has, however, made it clear to our community that Whitworth and Gonzaga are partners in a common goal of making Spokane a great place to go to college. We will both win.

Aggressiveness

Clichés are bad. Sports clichés are really bad. Generally, they don't mean anything, and the ones that do don't apply to life. Yesterday I heard, "We had to suck it up because our backs were against the wall." That's a strange image. Having been involved in athletics my whole life, I have to admit that one axiom does apply in some team sports: "The best offense is a good defense." The saying does not, however, apply to leadership. Good leaders want the ball. There aren't too many highly successful business ventures that were built on playing defense. Early researchers found aggressiveness to be a trait present in most leaders. The term "aggressiveness," as used by Bass represents a collection of qualities such as persistence, initiative, and ambition (1990, 68).

Too often, people in positions of leadership get bogged down trying not to make mistakes. We can certainly be very aggressive in defending our organizations or ourselves, but the best leaders channel their aggressiveness toward reaching their goals. The really aggressive ones love to score. Pitchers' duels are boring; these leaders want to see balls flying out of the park.

The twenty-first century, however, greeted unbridled aggressiveness in a very unfriendly manner. Wall Street punished the companies who bet everything on future earnings, those who didn't believe there was any point of diminishing returns on aggressiveness. The bandits at Enron, Global Crossings, Arthur Anderson, and even Fannie Mae failed to get away with aggressive accounting. Every virtue taken to excess becomes a fatal weakness. Aggressiveness must always be practiced in a way that recognizes the tension it's creating. Aggressiveness usually narrows our vision, which is not bad—we call that focus—but it also creates tension on people, tasks, or goals that compete for its energy. A whole pack of dot.com cowboys charged relentlessly after market shares, leaving behind an important companion—profitability. Our aggressiveness will work best with a wide angle lens that keeps all the variables in view.

Going fast is fun, and we get to our destinations sooner than if we plod along. I do like speed, but it can be dangerous. When I'm in a really aggressive mode, I'm energized and focused; that's when I'm least likely to hear voices other than the ones in my head. Recently, I set out to solve a nagging problem that was draining energy and resources from our university. I put my head down, plowed through the obstacles and got it done as quickly as possible. I also failed to hear a trusted colleague's very important questions on the matter. Looking back, by speeding through the problem I did more harm than good. I didn't recognize the tension my aggressiveness was creating.

Our organizations will fail to reach their potential without aggressiveness. Whether it be the plugging away of the tortoise or the darting of the hare, we must push hard. I try to always compliment aggressive mistakes, encouraging my coworkers that those are the best kind. As leaders, we need to model aggressiveness, but we absolutely must be sensitive to the tensions we're creating. Aggressive moves get us closer to our goals, but they also get us closer to breakpoints we can ill afford.

ENERGY

Energy is a strange force when viewed in isolation. Physicists and philosophers agree that energy has no intrinsic moral property. My dad felt differently. Two of my sixth-grade friends were Rodney the hell-raiser and Danny the docile. After I'd oozed my way home following an afternoon of TV and potato chips with Danny, my dad greeted me with, "How come you haven't been hanging out with Rodney lately?" I was incredulous. Less than a month earlier, I'd arrived home from a little-league game to a chalkboard note that read, "Billy, we have gone to prayer meeting. You are to go to the police station and ask for Sergeant Pete Anderson." Grrr. I had submitted myself to Rodney's leadership once too often. So, thinking my cleric father had either lost his memory or decided my best occupational bet was crime, I simply replied, "Rodney?" Dad muttered as he walked away, disgusted with his sodden son, "At least he has energy." That's when I discovered that Dad wasn't kidding when he would bark, "Do something, even if it's wrong!"

Few of the early researchers tested energy as a correlate of leadership, but the ones who did found that most leaders had plenty of the stuff. Further studies confirmed the findings. When Bass surveyed the research between 1948 and 1970, he found "25 studies—many more than the 1948 survey—which suggested that the leader tends to be endowed with an abundant reserve of energy, stamina and ability to maintain a high rate of physical activity" (1990, 81).

A good leader can create energy in the organization without always supplying it. In December 1985, syndicated columnist Mark Shields published a column that argued Ronald Reagan had outperformed Jimmy Carter in the presidency because Reagan himself supplied less direct energy to his office. Shields used an interesting model to make his case:

> Nearly five years into his presidency, Ronald Reagan has again recast the chief executive's job, this time somewhat after a model used by the turn-of-the-century German general staff. In searching for its future commanders, the leadership of the German army put every officer into one of four groups. The first were the dumb and the lazy, who were going nowhere. Second were the dumb and the energetic (clearly the most troublesome subgroup in all human organizations). Third were the bright and the energetic, who were passed over for the command assignments but who were thought to make the best staff people. The command posts were to go to those in the fourth group—the bright and the lazy—who were deemed most capable of figuring out the easiest as well as the most sensible means of accomplishing an objective. (1985, A19)

Shields went on to observe, "Jimmy Carter was obviously bright and relentlessly energetic, while Ronald Reagan is bright, if less obviously so, and not given to bragging about long hours in the office." This lighthearted comparison points to the difference between a leader being the fount of energy and a leader being the catalyst of energy.

In the utilities industry, energy is converted into power. In organizational life, power is converted into energy. Ronald Reagan delegated power, not just responsibility, and that power created energy. I believe one of the reasons the U.S. economy soared in the nineties was because during the last half of the eighties our country's flagship companies pushed power closer to the customer. The woman at the counter and the guy at the cash register got new jobs. They became problem-solvers and decision-makers rather than vacant bureaucrats. This movement injected energy into the heart of the American worker while freeing general managers to become strategists rather than high-paid operators.

I think leaders should personify energy. One of the few things in life we can totally control is our effort. I love the rush of busting my tail, whether it's at work or play. At eleven o'clock on a Saturday night I sent an e-mail to a friend of mine who is president of the University of Washington. I can't remember what it was about, but I remember smiling when the reply came instantaneously. He was at his desk. I suspect we had both gotten home from some event and still had a little gas in our tanks. I will admit that part of our energy quotient shows up in how we feel. Some days I wake up with the zeal of a slug. But I also believe that energy is a choice that leaders must make, and the more often they choose it, the less often the slug shows up.

LEADING FROM THE MIDDLE

Desire to excel. If there is a sine qua non of leadership success, it is probably the desire to excel. It is a commitment that must penetrate every corner of our organizations. It must be modeled, proclaimed, and distributed. It must be crystal clear to both our customers and our employees, but this desire must also be regulated. The modeling, proclaiming, and distributing of our desire to excel are not done well from a distance. They are done best when our people are in a position to see our commitment, to hear us when we speak in a normal voice, and to volunteer to join in the cause. Our commitment to excellence is communicated better when we help move the chairs around to make the room just right than when we send an e-mail to the physical-plant employees about our standards. Customers, as well, best see our insistence on excellence when we move in their midst, peppering them with questions on how we can improve.

Leading from the middle of the pack also reminds us just how much the pack wants to excel. We see the deft work of our specialists, whose knowledge of their areas underscores our reliance on their skill. Leaders are not only in a better position to empower from the middle,

87

they are also inspired by the good work of the coworkers who support them and stand ready for more responsibility.

Aggressiveness. Few leadership traits need to be "surrounded" as much as aggressiveness. Leading from the middle of the mission and the people is the safest spot for the aggressive leader. Constant contact with the mission will protect a leader from the kind of opportunism that seduces organizational jet pilots. One could probably make the case that it was aggressiveness that made Nixon-adviser-turned-convict-turned-Christian-apologist Chuck Colson very valuable to the president, and excessive aggressiveness landed him in jail. When Colson got out of prison, he started Prison Fellowship. In those early years, I helped out as a consultant for the program. When the organization was small, it grew by opportunity as much as by mission. As it got larger and Chuck had more opportunities, the organization went through a bit of an identity crisis. Eventually, Chuck got himself in the middle of the organization, surrounded himself with mission-driven people, and managed from there instead of from out in front. Since then, the Prison Fellowship has flourished, and Chuck's aggressiveness has been focused on the right things.

If we're going to make mistakes of aggressiveness, we better have folks around us who can anticipate what our focus blinds us from seeing—people who know us well enough to warn us and redirect us a few degrees; people who will pick us up when we fall. We need to be in a position to hear these people.

The final reason aggressiveness works best in the middle of one's mission and people is that it is from the middle that a leader's enthusiasm best rubs off on the corporate culture. I push our mission hard. Not everyone at our university agrees with what I do, but no one will deny that I'm aggressive about our mission. The mission aggressiveness that people see firsthand has helped convert a written statement into a shared set of values. James Kouzes and Barry Posner make their case for the impact of shared values in reporting a study that found companies with corporate cultures based on a foundation of shared values "outperformed other firms by a huge margin" (1997, 215). At our last comprehensive regional accreditation visit, I greeted the team of ten evaluators with, "Let me do with you what I do with all visitors and tell you about our distinctive mission." The twenty-some people in the room from our university had to be thinking, *Here comes the broken record.* But in my exit interview with the team's chair, she reported never having been at a school with such a shared sense of mission. A leader's aggressiveness will invariably be positive when leading takes place from the middle of the mission and of the people.

Energy. The first person I ever saw lead from the middle is still my best example of what it means. I could have used him for a model for every leadership trait, but he was really good at generating energy by staying in the midst of his people. I was twenty-two years old when I met John Thatcher, owner and president of the company his late father started, Yes Banana Supply Inc., in Miami, Florida. John was a man of towering integrity whose lunch pail overflowed with the loaves and fishes of virtue that absolutely energized his employees. John was exactly twice as old as I when we met. When I would stop by his office to say hello or to meet him for golf, he'd deliver a ritual homily on the physical, moral, social, and spiritual benefits of the banana. My, how he believed in his product! Then, on those lucky days when he didn't have a bunch in his office, we would head for the yard in pursuit of the yellow torpedoes that John believed shot right into the soul with all that is right and good. Those walks through the yard imprinted me forever with a picture of how I wanted to lead. To me, walking around the company with John felt like a victory march. When this man, born of privilege and stationed, almost without choice, in his father's vineyard, walked back among his loaders and truck drivers, he took on hero proportions.

I could never keep myself from commenting to John about how his people all seemed so purposeful in their work. Big smiles would cross their faces as they waved, shouting, "Hey, Mr. Thatcher," while darting wherever. John would always attribute their energy and dispositions to his having hired good people. As I got to know John, I discovered it was far more than that. I worked at John's church, having compromised my commitment to spend a year as a hobo in a warm climate after graduating in January from a college in the tundra region of the United States. One Sunday after church, John invited me to play golf at his country club. Having never golfed at a country club, I was slack-jawed at its opulence from the moment we arrived. So, of course, I asked John how often he golfed at this luxurious course. "Sunday afternoons if I'm lucky; that's it," he said ruefully. When I asked why he didn't play more often, he shrugged and said, "I don't think I should play golf when my people are working." It was at that point I knew what put bounce in the steps of the employees at Yes Banana Supply Inc.

Leaders need to think as much about the examples they set as the instructions they give. As we move into the midst of our people, the electric current becomes reciprocal. We create energy in them, and they create energy in us. Leaders must realize that the lunchroom can generate as much energy as the boardroom.

REFLECTION
REACTING (THE FIRST RESPONSE)

Hard-driving leaders tend to keep their engines revved at very high RPM levels. They're lucky to even notice the roses you're supposed to stop and smell. These folks are not always in the perfect frame of mind to greet difficult surprises as carefully and deliberately as they might. And, whether they like it or not, everyone is watching. They're taking their cues from the leader. I've found that the first response of the person in charge to almost any situation is like an entrance to a highway express lane. You can't exit; you can't turn back; you're on your way to wherever it's going.

I've learned this rule from failed attempts to backtrack and from a couple of successes. In December 1995, our family set off to spend Christmas with my sister and her family in Caracas, Venezuela. A snowstorm in Chicago rerouted us through Miami, where I had lived in my single days. Taking advantage of a five-hour layover, I rented a car and decided to take my family to the beach where I hung out years back. After a thirty-minute walk by the water, we returned to the car. I got there about a minute before Bonnie and the kids. What I found was a broken window and a burglarized car. Our carry-ons, the money the kids had saved, our son's new camera, our tickets, passports, the works—all were stolen.

As the family approached the scene, somehow my anger was interrupted with the thought that our children would never forget the next five minutes, and my response to this mess would probably determine our attitudes toward all that would follow. Having that sixty-second lag time gave me a chance to think, rather than to react. How I interpreted the disaster to the family bore little resemblance to the rage I felt at the moment of discovery. Somehow, I found the words and tone to communicate comfort rather than anger. I'm sure I remember my self-control because it contrasted with my usual knee-jerk emotional reactions, and because I had to control my knee a few more times when I remembered that the federal government had shut down for the day, and with it the passport offices.

Eventually, we made it to South America with the disaster put well behind us. As I have been faced with crises and surprises since then, I haven't forgotten the value of that lag time I used to gather myself. I have also discovered that the availability of lag time doesn't have to be controlled by circumstances. If we spend the first moments absorbing after encountering bad news, unfair accusations, horrible situations, or any big surprise, we can create a bracket of think-time before responding. Personally, thinking always improves the way I deal with a situation. Duh.

I know there are times when we botch our initial handling of difficult situations. I've sent a few ugly memos I wish I had back. Apologizing to offended parties, changing courses, and confessing our sins of overreaction are better ways to handle dumb responses than digging in to the bitter end. Sometimes we're wrong, and the odds of being wrong are greater when we don't have, or take, time to think.

Passing a twenty-four-hour law has helped me. When I learn of a situation that upsets me, any nonurgent decision or response I make has to be discussed with a cabinet member, then delayed twenty-four hours. Besides putting my mind back in charge of my tongue, I have found that the twenty-four-hour cooling time doesn't alter most of the situations that I thought needed my instant response. Sometimes we get into an umpire mentality and feel we need to holler something immediately. I hate it when I realize that I sat on a decision for a week without getting any new information. I hate it worse when I discover after a week that a situation looks much different than it did when I made my snap response. The mental reflex of absorbing before responding helps avoid the latter.

Traits Related to Personality

I have made the claim that traits related to effort rest more on choice than traits related to personality. Someday geneticists may prove that claim to be false. It may be that aggressive, energetic people who seek have an "effort gene" lighting a fire in their DNA. But originality, popularity, humor, and sociability seem to be more directly related to a person's fundamental personality than how hard the person pursues his or her goals.

It might be that personality traits would fascinate me less had I not been born in 1949. I first heard the term "charisma" in reference to John F. Kennedy. I am certain that at no other time in U. S. history were sixth graders claiming that one presidential candidate was "all charisma." But in my little GOP town, JFK had too much charisma to be trusted (plus, our parents were telling us we'd be electing the pope as president). I then watched Martin Luther King, Jr. rally millions of people by infusing a moral cause with his captivating personality. It could well be that the course of history turned in the 1960s on the strength of personality-based leadership.

It would be a mistake to think the following four personality traits are indispensable elements of leadership. I see them rather as facilitators. It would also be wrong to think you either have them or you don't just because they may be somewhat less controllable than traits related to effort. All four of these traits are worth developing, no matter where we start.

Originality

I can't say that everything I needed to know about life I learned in kindergarten, but I can say that one of my great lessons in originality took place in a kindergarten boys' room. It was spring of my senior year in high school and I had landed the job of janitor at my old elementary school. Head custodian Dick Lau was taking me on a tour of my duties, showing me my job description. As we were working our way down the kindergarten/first-grade hall, we turned into the boys' room. I remembered it as the one place Miss Rimshus learned to let me visit on demand. Two steps into my old haven, I knew Dick Lau was a creative genius. Eighteen inches off the floor, painted right in the center of the white porcelain urinals, were brightly colored bulls eyes. "Yeah, Bill, back when you were a kid you guys would start peein', then some kid would give you shove or tell you to look at his rabbit's foot and you'd spin around like a dang lawn sprinkler. The day I painted those bulls' eyes is the day I stopped cleaning pee off every wall in this room." I don't know if I can hold this up as the kind of original leadership we need in the twenty-first century, but here's one guy who had to color outside the lines to get little boys to pee inside the toilets.

If I never again hear the term "paradigm shift," it will be too soon. But I have to admit, no matter how tired I might be of this trendy term, it is undeniable that the twenty-first century will require its leaders to think in very different ways than business as usual. Valuing originality in the way we see our tasks will unlock creativity among all with whom we work. A leader must either possess or recognize originality to survive in a relentlessly changing society. Here's an example:

While I was writing this book, I went to a Lowe's hardware store to buy a couple of cotter pins and nuts for the propeller shaft on our boat. I had lost the ones I removed after backing the boat into the side of our garage and bending the propeller. I did measure the size of the shaft, but I didn't write that down because I'm dumb enough to think that if I remembered to buy what I'd lost, I would also remember whether to get a 5/8- or 9/16-inch nut. But I didn't, so I bought two different-size cotter pins and two different-size nuts.

When I got to the counter with these four items and a hedge-trimmer (which I went on to wield with swashbuckling fervor, ruthlessly severing enemy branches, along with the power cord and part of my shin), the young clerk asked me if I had noticed the cost of my small items that had come from equally small bins. I had not. He looked at his phone, looked at the people in line behind me, then looked at me and said, "Take a guess." I said, "Three bucks all together." "Deal," he said, and twenty seconds later I was out of there.

Naturally, neither nut was the right size, so I had to go back and try again. I breezed in the next week, assumed the most "I'm in a hurry" look I could muster, and went straight to the service counter. In a sentence I explained my situation. "No problem," said the hardware man. "Just go back there and put back the ones you bought and get yourself the right ones." I asked if I needed to go through the checkout line. "Nah, you're fine," he said.

Do you have any idea how many old-school business conventions were violated in these two encounters? I can scarcely express how impressed I was that my time, other customers' time, and the compensated time of employees mattered more than a potential one-dollar mistake, which might have been in *their* favor. Then, to top it all off, I was trusted when I returned—another timesaving device.

Somebody at Lowe's gets a gold star for innovative thinking. I can almost see the big shots gasping when a company leader whispers the wild new idea: "Let's build a system and culture where we trust our employees, give them some authority, and trust our customers." The audacity!

What is it that makes us believe that in a world of exponential change, we can survive without creative, original thinking? In looking at subsequent eras of leadership, you'll find that the person in a leadership *position* doesn't need to be the source of originality. But the person at the top of the heap (usually the president, depending on whether it's the big heap or a sub-heap) has the broadest view of the problem. When the original thinking comes from the top position holder, it benefits from an expansive perspective as well as a "leader's nudge" inherent in the idea.

I use several questions to help stimulate my own original thinking:

- What is my desired ultimate outcome in this situation?

- Is my first answer really my desired outcome, or is there a greater one?

- What would I do if I were starting absolutely from scratch?

- What would I do if I had no new resources, limited resources, or unlimited resources?

- How would I think about this situation differently if I had to defend my ideas with our five-year plan?

Generally, my failures to think creatively can be traced to looking down instead of out. The other day I heard someone say that the difference between an introverted nerd and an extroverted nerd is that the introvert looks at his own shoelaces and the extrovert looks at the shoelaces of the person he's talking to. Sometimes that's about how far I lift my sights in strategic thinking. I forfeit the advantage of my position by taking short, narrow views. It's lazy thinking, and my employer can't afford it from me. I may not be the most original thinker on the team, but I need to be the most original thinker that I'm capable of being. And I also need to invite and reward creativity from other team members.

POPULARITY

My first glimpse into early twentieth century organizational life came during my junior year in a Chicago high school. I found out about my hometown's meatpacking industry when Mr. Beauprez made us read Upton Sinclair's *The Jungle*. Sinclair's novel did not exactly present an "I'm OK you're OK" work environment. I recall reading about a rather despotic supervisor who didn't even fish out the poor guy who fell into a sausage vat, figuring that the well-fed banker woofing down hot dogs on the corner of LaSalle and Madison would never know the difference. I became a sixteen-year-old vegetarian. Popularity didn't seem to matter much to "leaders" in *The Jungle*, but it did surface as an early twentieth century leadership trait.

I suspect popularity correlated with leadership in the minds of workers because of their failure to differentiate a popular leader from an effective leader. A clear definition of leadership was even more AWOL then versus now, but according to the literature in the field, workers felt the leaders seemed to be the more popular guys. (Almost all of the studies had only males as subjects.)

Few of us today would claim that a necessary connection exists between popularity and effective leadership. In athletics, effective leadership has a very quantifiable definition: wins and losses. As I mentioned, I'm from Chicago. During the nineties, a very unpopular citizen in the city was Bulls General Manager Jerry Krause. A former Bulls head coach told a friend of mine that Michael Jordan had "No lunches with Jerry Krause" written into his contract. That's unpopular. Nobody except Jerry Reinsdorf, Krause's boss, liked the guy. But the Bulls owned the NBA in the nineties. If nothing else, Krause was effective. A decade earlier, there was a Chicago businessman in a different neighborhood than Chicago Stadium named Jim Bere, CEO of Borg Warner. Everybody in the city adored the man, and Borg Warner employees were his biggest fans. Bere epitomized the popular, effective leader. Both Krause and Bere were effective, but they differed enormously in popularity.

I've heard many leaders say, "I couldn't care less how popular I am. My job is to create productivity." Personally, I don't disconnect popularity from productivity quite so easily. I think popularity is very helpful in exercising effective leadership. Certainly, trust and respect trump popularity, but being popular, especially among those whom you have been charged to lead, provides a leader with higher levels of acceptance and margin in an organization. Folks grant a little more grace for people they like. My senior year in high school, I was voted "most popular" in the yearbook sweepstakes. I knew I'd get it. I was the only kid out of the 331 seniors who had a strategy to get it. The year before, I'd been voted student body president using the same strategy. I knew the name of every human being in our school, and never once failed to say "Hi" and add the person's name upon encounter. I sounded like an auctioneer on speed when a group of ten or more students walked by. I turned out to be one of the worst student body presidents in anyone's memory, but at least I was popular … at first.

The expanded acceptance and margin provided by being liked serve more as bonuses than necessities. I could sit at the controls of my university and make things work OK, but I feel advantaged when students and workers actually welcome me when I show up. When I eat in the dining commons, I often sit down with a table of students whom I don't know well or don't know at all. It's hard to overstate how much I've learned from these times listening to students. I feel the same welcome and benefit walking into the physical plant and sparring playfully with folks there. Being relatively approachable helps leaders gauge and influence the organizational climate.

Becoming a popular leader presents a bit more of a challenge than showing that big smile in your high-school yearbook. I've thought about this quite a bit. What are the keys? There probably are no keys that can substitute for transparently loving the people we work with, but it still helps to assume a certain mindset when we set foot in the workplace. My basic advice for those who feel the need to raise their popularity quotient is so simple it's almost insulting to mention; but here it is: try.

Think about the dedication and effort of the people you lead. Think about the honor it is to be liked by these people. Think about what you can do not only to earn their respect, but to also earn their affection. The answer will be different for all of us, but the question is worth asking: why should my people like me? Then, try to be liked. You may need to drop the symbols that remind people of your exalted position. Sometimes expensive dresses, neckties and impressive titles have to be set aside. You might even spare your geography-bound employees from a recitation of your travel itinerary and all the important people you've just seen. Instead, ask a few questions about their families and jobs. Showing that you care will go a long way toward making you a popular leader.

HUMOR

This is the kind of trait that reminds us correlation tests identify only coexistence, not causality. I haven't seen too many pictures of Abraham Lincoln caught in the middle of a belly laugh, and I wouldn't call Pee Wee Herman a leader. A sense of humor doesn't create leadership, but it probably helps. Humor made Bass's list because the few studies that correlated leadership with humor revealed pretty high correlation coefficients. The definitions of humor vary, but it's pretty clear that some kind of lightheartedness can be found in most leaders. In at least one of the studies Bass reviewed, laughter was the activity measured as representing humor, and leaders did more laughing than group members (Bass 1990, 70). Maybe being a leader is funny.

My primary observation about humor has little to do with jokes. The humor that best serves leaders springs from their ability to laugh at themselves. A leader who doesn't take himself or herself too seriously wears an approachability that solemn leaders might desire but have a hard time communicating. Countenance counts. We underestimate the communication value of the persona we put on. I have nine people who report to me directly (too many unless you really like the middle) with whom I meet weekly. One of the most important things we do is laugh. We are all willing to trade stiffly efficient meetings for a few yuks.

Working with students begs for jocularity. Our language exposes the industry. Take "sophomore," for instance. The root of "moron" is preceded by the root of "sophistry," a derisive term referring to the ceaseless drivel that came from the mouths of a pompous group of empty-headed, pseudo-intellectual Greek philosophers. Hence, the denotation of sophomore is a "babbling pseudo-intellectual moron," an oft times apt moniker. Sometimes I find the only alternative to eternal discouragement is wondrous laughter. And that's not so hard because students are fun. Regularly, I spar with them, and they with me. It reduces the distance between us.

Laughing easily not only makes leaders more approachable by humanizing them, it can also give power to our more serious messages. As I indicated in Chapter Two's discussion of paradoxical leadership, contrast increases impact. Early Greek theatre often juxtaposed comedy and tragedy in very powerful ways. I received an e-mail from someone who commented on the impact of this contrast in reference to the opening paragraph of my monthly newsletter that read:

> Here's my situation. I'm not on a plane. I'm sitting on the deck at our cabin. Before me a perfectly still river reflects tree-topped mountains as a rising sun delivers warmth through the cool, early morning air. Surrounded by the splendor of God's creation, one question dominates my thoughts, "I wonder how we're doing on the general education curriculum." I need professional help. Actually, before I started fussing, the beauty of the earth did seem to enrich my morning prayers. Among those prayers was intercession on behalf of a wonderful friend in Portland battling the return of a virulent cancer. Please pray for her. Life is, at once, so good and so hard. I find its joys and sorrows seem to be intensifying. Maybe I'm getting more emotional as I age; or maybe Bonnie's sensitivity is rubbing off on me.

I heard that she cried at the grand opening of Alton's Tire Center. Well, I hope you are having a renewing summer season. Even when we're working hard, the change of rhythm in the academic calendar refreshes us at Whitworth.

This isn't, by a long shot, great writing. But sandwiching heartbreak between lighthearted comments can be done in a way that keeps us from being maudlin without trivializing our sadness. Sometimes life is funny; sometimes it's sad. Being able to laugh and cry is just human.

I'm not going to spend many more words on the subject of humor other than to claim that leaders lead better when they lighten up. Sometimes, laughing is the difference between a leader being perceived as on the ball or aloof. I don't really want our employees to perceive me as being bogged down by the pressures of my work. It creates unnecessary anxiety in the organization. Nor do I want an air of immunity that presents me as untouchable. Like everyone else, I have a job, I have a personal life, and there is joy to be found in both.

SOCIABILITY

I don't have too much to say about sociability, partly because I'm not sure what the researchers who identified it as a leadership trait really found, other than something they loosely called social skills. In this respect, sociability differs from popularity, which is located in the esteem of the group, and may or may not be based on social skills.

There were eight studies between 1915 and 1944 that found a strong connection between sociability and leadership, but most of these studies were performed on children (1990, 72). I pay no attention to children who lead, unless they're armed. I think for the most part, the bossiest kids elbow their way into becoming the class CEO. When Rodney transferred into our sixth grade and smacked me after I questioned his mutinous suggestion that we do things his way rather than my way, I found his argument convincing. I'm not going to make too many major changes in my leadership because of what researchers learned about eleven year olds in 1932 who were voted "leaders" by their gang members.

I would have skipped this vague finding of sociability were it not for its proximity to a dimension of social perception that seems to make a huge difference in how people think about one another. Vintage research by social psychologist Solomon Asch offers leaders a compelling identification of one influential prism through which people are perceived socially.

During the same period that leadership styles were pushing aside trait thinking, Asch conducted studies in impression formation that suggested that certain characteristics dominated the way a person's other attributes were perceived.

In one of his most famed studies, Asch took six characteristics— intelligent, skillful, industrious, determined, practical, and cautious— then placed "cold" or "warm" in the middle of the list. To one group in his experiment he gave the list of six traits with "cold" in the middle and to the other group he gave the same list but substituted "warm" for "cold." He then had members of each group describe the person with the seven characteristics. The descriptions couldn't have been more different, stirring up images that ranged from Warm Ozzie Nelson to Cold Al Capone. "Warm" and "cold" proved to be traits that sent folks down two very different perceptual paths.

If we grant sociability as a leadership trait, this research suggests we should build on a foundation of warmth. I don't think all the heat must be on the surface, but somewhere in the leader's personage there needs to be a warmth that advocates for the rest of his or her attributes. Evidently, warmth serves as a broker of grace in how we are perceived by those who make contact with us.

My challenge with warmth and with sociability in general is the influence that situations have over my moods. I trapeze my way between charming and distant as the situational winds blow. I hate that about myself. Not ten minutes into my assistant's interview for her job, I found myself apologizing in advance for my inevitable insensitivity.

But I'm improving by doing a few things:

- First, I've convinced myself of the importance of being warm, even when I don't feel warm.

- Second, I've convinced myself that others do not necessarily interpret my warmth as an invitation for them to ask me about my personal life, or worse, tell me about theirs.

- Third, I'm trying to make situations work for me instead of against me. I slam myself into situations that melt the ice left over from whatever had thrown me into my arctic mood. Usually, a connection with students, my children or a couple of goofy friends can whip me into shape.

In some loosely defined way, sociability surfaced as a leadership trait in the early studies. At the minimum, it seems to tint the glasses people put on when looking at leaders. While it isn't the nucleus of leadership, sociability does seem to have some facilitating value to leading others.

LEADING FROM THE MIDDLE

Creativity. The questions I use to stir my creative juices are helpful, but I'm not really one who bleeds creativity. I think my greater strength is doing scenario thinking in a way that analyzes the outcomes of new ideas. That being the case, I need to rely on others for originality. The biggest advantage of leading from the middle with respect to creativity is that it is the best position from which to solicit and hear creative ideas and solutions. At the end of every summer, my wife and I host a picnic lunch for the college's physical-plant workers, mainly to say thanks for their hard work. After lunch, the VP to whom the physical plant reports and I always ask these workers for ideas on how we can improve our campus or our operations. We give little prizes for the best ideas and make a big deal out of it. The physical plant people love it and they always deliver great suggestions. I find that when I get in the middle of our people, I hear very clever ideas, ones that don't seem to find their way to my office.

Popularity. I think it was some automobile manufacturer that coined the slogan, "The closer you look, the better we look." I think that's true of good people. They are usually well liked by others, "once you get to know them." We all have stories about getting to know a high-profile person and discovering, "She was really a nice person. I liked her." Early in my academic life, I was leased from my college by Bell and

Howell Inc. to consult full-time in one of the companies they owned. After I'd made my first presentation to a group convened by Mr. Frey, the venerated Bell and Howell chairman of the board, he walked up and startled me by saying, "You don't come across as one of those head-up-your-ass academics I expected." I startled myself by replying, "You don't come across as the nasty son-of-a-bitch I expected." Fortunately, he found that funny and it paved the way for me to get to know him pretty well. He was far from the square-jawed bottom-liner that people who didn't know him said he was. In fact, universally, those closest to him said the better they knew him, the more they liked him. Leading from among the people allows us to be known and liked by the people we serve. That doesn't mean we have to be buddies; it just means we have the confidence in our coworkers to step out from behind our positions.

Humor. Certainly, the middle of the organization welcomes a leader's levity, but additionally humor presents leaders with a *pathway* to the middle. Laughter's reputation as the universal language is well deserved. That same universality provides laughter with an equalizing quality that reduces the distance between and among those who burst into it. Laughter reminds us of our common humanity. Light-hearted self-deprecation is a good way to get ourselves off our high horses. I believe firmly that all employees become marksmen when they see their leaders riding too high. Our choice is whether we climb off the horse or get shot off.

Sociability. The principal advantage provided by the middle in the area of sociability accrues particularly to less outgoing leaders. Some people don't lead with their warmth, but they have affirming social skills that unfold as a relationship develops. They are people who truly care about others. Leaders with sociability that lies beneath the surface do well to put themselves in a position for people to see past the veneer.

REFLECTION
THE ANSWER IS THE QUESTION

How does a president stay knowledgeable about the university, show concern for the employees, ward off self-delusion, and keep from becoming a bore? Answer: by being the number-one question asker on campus. I've worked on this for twenty years, I've improved significantly, and I'm still not very good.

My lessons on the value of maintaining an inquisitive mindset have come from morning-after remorse. My wife, Bonnie, loves me enough to provide me with end-of-the-evening ratios of my holding forth to my asking questions whenever I get obnoxious. I begin to loathe myself during her silent period, which begins the moment we are alone and which she breaks only when I ask for the ugly results of the evening.

Getting assaulted with the truth is bad; having to ask for the assault is worse. But my periods of reform are worth the pain. I do get into an inquisitive frame of mind that invites information from others, which is far more valuable to me than listening to the dull din of what I already know.

Being a question asker can be gimmicky if you think of it as a technique rather than an attitude. At every level, leaders need to learn and to model learning. Neither organizations nor the workers within organizations are static. Supervisors must constantly probe if they are to stay current with their people. When we ask a question, we compliment our coworkers with a metamessage, which says, "You know something that I would like to learn."

Leaders need to think about customers, coworkers, and other constituents as sources of abundant information and perspective. Usually, a simple question will unlock this rich resource. A mindset of inquisitiveness benefits everyone.

SUMMARY OF TRAIT-BASED LEADERSHIP FINDINGS

Leaders in the first part of this century held certain characteristics in common. Admittedly, the researchers who identified these traits often had a rather long bridge to cross in taking what they learned from children, gangs, and even the military, and applying it to leaders in general. We should not, however, dismiss their work as naïve discoveries in the adolescence of leadership studies. I find peril in distrusting the first impressions of a major research effort. The claim that most leaders have certain qualities passes the intuition test. Undeniably, leaders who enter the race with the fundamental properties of commitment to excellence, originality, popularity, aggressiveness, humor, energy, and social sensitivity will enjoy a significant tailwind.

Although I respect their work in identifying these qualities, I do not consider these traits to be genetically determined. I will admit to predispositions that make their development more or less likely, but to assume they can be neither lost nor found contradicts our experience. These qualities serve as facilitators in the exercise of leadership. To view them as generic breeds overconfidence for the haves and hopelessness for the have-nots.

The leadership characteristics I reviewed grow and spread well in the garden of the middle. When surrounded by coworkers in pursuit of a common goal, leaders and followers inspire the qualities in one another that propel them toward that goal. My spirits get me off kilter so easily that I become very brisk and diffident. What gets me back on course is being clocked by the loving, velvet-covered two-by-four upside my head, delivered by some gesture or action from the wonderful people with whom I live and work. We need to stay close to each other.

Chapter Nine

Style-Based Leadership

Leadership theory, over the course of the last century, has shifted the perceived epicenter of effectiveness away from what the leader wants and toward what the group needs. In the move from traits to style, this shift is subtle. A close look reveals two ways in which the centrality of the leader began to slip. First, "style" referred to a quality that was more changeable and less inherent than traits. It was thought to be context specific and was driven by a way of thinking more than by personality. Although theorists believed that leaders possessed "preferred styles," style represented an assumable approach to management, not characteristics that marked a person across relationships. For example, two leaders with similar levels of originality, humor, aggressiveness, and energy could find themselves at opposite ends of the democratic-autocratic style continuum.

Another basis for my argument that styles represents a move away from the leader and toward the led comes from a broad look at the subsequent stages. Although overlapping, the stages in leadership studies moved from traits, to styles, to certain behaviors from anyone in the group, and finally to the leader and the group engaged in mutually adaptive action toward the achievement of a common goal. I think it was the shift from traits to style that led the way for the diffusion of leadership throughout the group.

Clearly, the designated leader becomes more of a cultivator than a fountain of direct leadership as we move through the century.

During this period in which scholars focused on leadership styles, researchers began to discover that the success of certain approaches to leadership was influenced heavily by situational factors. In the first college where I worked, our chief financial officer often made the claim, "A good manager can manage anything." It's possible that he was trying to convince himself, as this was his first job in education, but I think he believed his axiom. Silly me, I thought you had to know something about your product. If we define management strictly in terms of directing the execution of operations, then my friend might have been right. Situational theorists, however, would contend that whether a leader is good or not can't be determined in a vacuum.* Situations exert strong influence over the effectiveness of a particular style.

The early situational researchers (pre-1960) theorized about the relationship between leaders' traits and their effectiveness. An intriguing question for all students of this connection was whether a certain kind of leader was the cause or the effect of a situation (Bass 1990, 38). In other words, did the situation bring out the right set of traits in a leader, or did the leader with the right set of traits get drawn into the situation? Generating these kinds of questions paved the way for the voluminous work of the situation/contingency theorists that followed.

Many researchers have theorized, during and since this period, about how leadership style and situation interact. The majority of the studies examined the circumstances under which either a task-oriented style or a relationship-oriented style would function best. Chapter Ten of Gary Yukl's *Leadership in Organizations* gives an excellent overview of the five dominant style-situation theories. For my purposes, I will focus on the way situation influences the effectiveness of the two most frequently examined style continuums: authoritarian/democratic and task/relationship.

---

* I have not emphasized the popular distinction between a "manager" and a "leader." Right smack on the cover of Bennis and Nanus's book, Leaders: Strategies for Taking Charge (1990 edition) appears, "Managers do things right, leaders do the right thing." The reasons I haven't touted this popular quote are (a) it artificially separates two overlapping roles, (b) it carries a condescending tone toward managers, (c) it's bad English, and (d) like most clichés, it commits the sin of oversimplification.

FINDINGS

Clearly, two style perspectives dominated the research during the middle of the twentieth century. Although countless styles were identified, the majority of them can find a place on one of two continuums:

Figure 1
Leadership Continuums

Authoritarian_____Democrat
(Group has little influence)   (Group has great influence)

Task-oriented_____Relationship-oriented

THE AUTHORITARIAN/DEMOCRATIC CONTINUUM

The first and perhaps most emotionally charged leadership style variable studied during this period was authority/democracy. How authoritarian or democratic should a leader be for optimum productivity? This research question raged during World War II, as democracy and socialism battled the forces of totalitarianism. In fact, it was a simple experiment with children that broke loose the avalanche of studies on authoritarianism that would follow. It was one of the most famed experiments in behavioral science history, and was conducted in America as Hitler was trampling Europe.

In 1939, Kurt Lewin engineered an experiment on children's playgroups from which he concluded that democracy was not only the most humane form of leadership but also the most effective (Lewin, Lippit, and White 1939). The study examined how children functioned under authoritarian leaders, democratic leaders, and laissez-faire leaders. To no one's surprise, the democratic leaders accomplished the most tasks and created the best morale, while the totalitarian leaders proved ineffective and demoralizing.

Although a strong case can be made for the truth of these findings, some researchers suggested that bias crept into the experimental design. Kurt Lewin, who was Jewish, left Germany in 1933. Watching his homeland drink the poison of Hitler's brand of authoritarianism could have influenced his perspective in a way that was understandable, if not predictable. This experiment, nevertheless, was the granddaddy of a new way to look at leadership.

Throughout the 1950s, behavioral scientists studied the influence of the authoritarian/democratic leadership variable. Rensis Likert's typology represents the typical research on the continuum (Likert 1961):

- **Authoritarian:** totally leader-centered.

- **Benevolent Authoritarian:** totally leader-directed, but with consideration for the group.

- **Consultative:** leader-refereed, making the final decision after consulting with the group.

- **Participative:** leader as convener/advisor but with no more decision-making power than other group members.

Parallel terms such as "teller, seller, consulter, joiner" refer to the same model (Tannebaum and Schmidt 1958). Whatever nomenclature one applies, the poles remain the same with leader-centered at one end and group-centered at the other. I prefer to think of the two poles as leadership pre-dispositions or orientations. Leaders tend to drift naturally in one direction or the other, but are not prisoners of a type. Clever differentiations, whether in leadership styles or personality types, sell very nicely but always get caught trying to force complex human beings into categories.

AUTHORITARIAN LEADERSHIP

I learned a great deal about how authoritarian leadership works during my presidencies at two different colleges.

At the first college, I was only the fourth president in seventy-five years. My predecessor had run things for thirty years and was clearly authoritarian. Although he did take into consideration how the campus community would receive his decisions, he didn't lose a lot of sleep over making a decision that nobody liked. Every nuance of his persona declared "I'm in charge." I would have killed for his voice. His "pass the salt and pepper" thundered through the room, causing all souls present to hope they might be the bearers of that salt and pepper. You wanted to stand and salute. I, on the other hand, arrived on the scene at age thirty-six feeling, by comparison, pimply and adolescent. When I gave orders and barked, "and I mean it!" somebody would yawn and pass me the salt and pepper.

In my second presidency, I was the fourth president in seven years, if you counted two interims. My predecessor had very successfully led another college for eleven years and made important, albeit difficult, moves in this, his second presidency. But reports were that he'd become somewhat withdrawn on a campus that was already quite decentralized in its governance and administration. It couldn't have been a more different situation than what had awaited me at my first presidency. Interestingly, this president also fit into the authoritarian classification, demonstrating the varying effects of mixing style with a leader's traits or with a particular situation. For example, my first predecessor involved himself directly in all the hiring and firing, personally making the offers or handing out the pink slips. My second predecessor gave his vice presidents orders, but detached himself from direct involvement with hiring and firing. Both leaders functioned in relatively autocratic ways, but they differed greatly in executing their decisions.

Although the authoritarian approach occupied the cellar of my favorite styles, history isn't as harsh with some authoritarian leaders. As I have just implied, it is important to note that style stands independent of the morality, wisdom and importance of a leader's goals. By current standards, almost all leaders of past eras functioned very autocratically. When I was growing up, my mother seemed to feel it important for me to be able to differentiate ancient Israel's good kings from the bad ones by their motives. I never thought to ask her whether Jeroboam donned a more participatory style than that rascal Rehoboam. Kings were kings. They were all autocrats.

I believe authoritarianism should refer only to a unilateral style, not to motive or intent (i.e. "benevolent"). As a style, this continuum should be based on the degree to which the people at large are involved in significant decisions. I think the entire human relations movement (McGregor, Argyris, Blake and Mouton, and others), who adored Likert's theories on participatory management, lobbied leadership researchers to put in a bad word for authoritarianism. Failing to distinguish between style and intent makes it difficult to look at authoritarianism objectively.

I am not, by a long shot, authoritarian in the way I lead, but I do not find the style necessarily bulging with self-interest. Although history is littered with egomaniacal political dictators, we also find those father-figure leaders who shepherd their people to safety, then turn to battle the wolves alone. Neither approach is very smart, in my opinion, but the latter abandons self-interest, authoritatively blocking followers' involvement. If we define "authoritarian" in a way that necessarily includes "lording" or "punishing," as did some researchers, then to conclude that authoritarianism is a bad style is redundant.

BENEFITS OF AUTHORITARIAN LEADERSHIP

Efficiency. An authoritarian leadership style usually functions at a higher level of efficiency than a democratic approach. I work in an industry that has this thing called "shared governance," which means the faculty gets to weigh in on relevant matters—i.e., all matters. Most presidents consider this need for faculty buy-in the bane of their existence. Actually, I don't mind it, but it is slow. Robert Siever of Stamats, Inc., likes to quote a recent *Fortune* magazine on what I do for a living:

> The CEO isn't free to run the business; he or she needs the workers' approval for most major decisions. The pressures of managing-by-compromise force most bosses to depart within four years. As Thomas Hobbes, the 17th-century English philosopher put it, their lives are nasty, brutish, and short. Welcome to the byzantine business of higher education. (Tully 1995)

Authoritarian leaders don't need votes, permission, or advice. They make up their minds and march.

Clarity. Authoritarianism pretty much takes the finger pointing out of organizational whodunit. The leader is who done it; now deal with it. A few years ago, our campus was squirming over problems related to freshman initiation. For 80 percent of the students, it represented a sacrosanct tradition. The other 20 percent were still processing why they would be welcomed to a Presbyterian college by being immersed, not sprinkled, in slime and other foreign matter. I decided to kill the practice unilaterally. I wasn't going to check with student government, our student life staff, or Mac Hall—where initiation had been lifted to an art form. I didn't avoid those groups out of fear of resistance; rather, I wanted to protect them from being accused by the 80 percent of selling out. Stupidly, I let myself get conned into giving the students one last chance at propriety. The following year was all peace and light, but eventually, the slime returned and initiation was sentenced to death democratically, evoking all the multidirectional blaming that could have been avoided had I not chickened out the first time.

Predictability. I confess to a certain annoyance with ideologues. I seem to have some dark need to profane their well-rehearsed creeds, even when I think they are right. What I like about them, however, is they don't cast too many surprise votes. Predictability, if not taken to the extreme, has value. The collective trust and coherence of any organization relies on the consistency of its leaders. When determining the basic directions, goals, and strategies of a group, if leadership is centralized in a single authoritarian person, predictability rises.

Perspective. Like most presidents, I can claim that every person who reports to me has greater expertise in his or her area than I do. However, what none of them has is the breadth of my perspective. I love Max DePree's metaphor of the leader as a jazz band conductor (DePree 1989). In addition to all the specific ways in which a jazz band conductor allows the musicians to shine, the metaphor also points to perspective. It is the responsibility of the conductor to blend parts into a whole, unified sound. Authoritarian leaders find themselves in strong positions to identify discordant activity. Beautiful work loses its value if it isn't harmonized with the organization as a whole. Organizations disintegrate when no one keeps an eye on the big picture. Authoritarian leaders seldom allow that to happen.

Authoritarian leaders can provide an antidote to the stress-arousing levels of ambiguity that often characterize organizations attempting to respond to their environments. When leadership is highly decentralized, different units can find themselves marching in different directions at a different pace. Further, the odds increase that members of the units will stick their heads over the fence and whine about "how green you guys have it" over in that pasture. I do suspect too many authoritarian leaders are set in their ways. Were that not the case, they wouldn't get nervous about distributing their authority to others. But when their ways are good ways, reliable patterns bring consistency to the organization.

LIABILITIES OF AUTHORITARIAN LEADERSHIP

Of course, authoritarian leadership has a definite downside. Among the liabilities are these four:

Tunnel vision. Leaders who keep only their own counsel can lose the ability to see both threats to and opportunities for their organizations. In his famed study on the danger of consensus, Irving Janis makes the argument that gigantic national blunders can be traced to "groupthink" (Janis 1972). Janis argues convincingly that when a group banishes dissent, classifying it as "naysaying," bad decisions follow.

Authoritarian leadership discourages dissent. When protests have no efficacy, there won't be too many volunteers to don the prophetic mantle. But not only is defense weakened by tunnel vision, advancement opportunities are lost to the silence of the front lines.

I have a friend who made millions of dollars because the man for whom she was secretary believed that neither she nor most others in the company were capable of coming up with a good idea. Well, she was. So the company she started with one other "dumb" employee made a ton of money that could have fattened the bank account of her authoritarian boss.

Loss of ownership. Probably the most obvious loss an organization feels under authoritarian leadership is investment. Top-down leadership can allow the employees down the line to feel automated. The employees just drive, lacking the excitement they might feel had they been given a voice in planning the trip.

My wife and I were members of a church in which the combustion of our pastor's disposition and theology flamed a strident autocracy. It was pretty much "my way or the highway." While trying to explain to the church's highest-ranking lay leader why we were leaving, it struck me. We weren't in *our* church; we were in *his* church. With no buy-in we decided to check out.

To the extent leaders depend on charges to implement organizational strategies, they will benefit from engaging those charges in the planning process. This involvement not only generates good ideas, but it inspires people to succeed. It acknowledges our recognition and respect of their role as stakeholders.

Less innovative thinking. I had an amazing experience a few years ago. Three guys who worked with me when I ran a camp in the late 1970s came out to Washington for a weekend. It was the first time that the three of us had gotten together since our camp days. As we sat around the dinner table embellishing the past, I recalled an all-camp simulation of the 1976 Olympics that turned out to be a great success.

One of the guys, now an oral surgeon, said, "What I remember most is when you called us in to help you figure out how to score events." He told about an idea he offered to which I apparently replied, "That's a great idea. You don't make very many suggestions, but when you do, they're really good." He went on to say that to this day, when shyness tries to keep him silent, he will hear the whisper of that encouragement.

Leaders cultivate innovation by building an environment that exalts creative thinking. Praising the thinker and implementing an idea ignites the chain reaction of ideas that freshens and improves the way we do business. When the authoritarian leader gives the impression, either real or imagined, that the suggestion box is unlocked only on insignificant occasions, both the box and the organization will rust. An authoritarian style can reduce workers to operators rather than thinkers.

Loss of motivation. In authoritarian-based organizations, motivation tends to be more external to the worker than in decentralized authority situations. Authoritarian leaders shoulder more responsibility for success and failure than in organizations where power is diffused. Motivation in enterprises with top-heavy authority relies on incentives more than on employee drive.

In 1961, Herbert Kelman published an excellent typology for understanding the motivational source of people's attitudes. A person can be persuaded (or motivated) out of coercion, identification, or internalization. Coercion refers to any power-based influence one person has over another. Identification is based on the attractiveness of, or the desire to please, the source of influence. Internalization occurs when a person believes in the substance of the influence, independent of the source's power or attractiveness.

A corporate culture shaped by authoritarian leadership often finds group members functioning largely out of compliance. The absence of choice creates willing victims rather than enthusiastic contributors. If compliance is the baseline motivation, people will continue to march even if they don't like the authority or the orders don't make sense to them. This kind of motivation robs individuals and organizations of the enthusiasm that results from people being able to choose the course that they believe is best. Authoritarian leadership can easily lead to compliance-based motivation.

SITUATIONS FAVORING AN AUTHORITARIAN STYLE

When fast action is needed. Twenty years ago, I was discussing leadership styles in a graduate course I was teaching. At the time, I leaned toward the point of view that authoritarian leadership always demoralized those being led. Faking openness, I asked if any class members could identify situations in which the authoritarian style worked best. A class member raised his hand and began his response with, "I'm a firefighter." I knew he had me. In some decisions, speed trumps perfection. The trick in these situations is making sure the most knowledgeable person serves as or informs the leader.

When the leader is clearly the expert. Some very interesting leadership models surfaced in the twenty-first century, high-technology, start-up companies. I have a couple of friends who developed technologies, then assembled organizations around their inventions. These kind of young and hungry entrepreneurs disdain convention. They are in a race that offers a prize only for first place. Start-up company leaders are usually the world's foremost, and sometimes only, authorities on their technology. They become friendly, frenetic, fun-loving dictators in their tiny companies. They are the experts, and democratic gestures waste time and energy. Burn rate is their timer, and usually it can only be reset by angel investors. Certainly, as their companies grow, their need for expertise will extend to capital acquisition, marketing, finance, and all areas related to commercialization and growth. At that point, these leaders will discover the difficulty of attracting expertise into a corporate culture of central authority. But for now, the founders are the experts, and they aren't scheduling too many company seminars on "helping employees self-actualize through empowerment."

When the big picture is needed. Occasions emerge during the life of an organization when the individual units find themselves locked in a series of zero-sum relationships. In times of retrenchment, often the only way the resources of one unit can be strengthened is by reducing those of another. It is asking an awful lot of managers to strip themselves of all biases and determine what's best for the good of the whole. Armed with the strategic plan and a clear commitment to the mission, the authoritarian leader will make good-of-the-organization decisions, and in the process will emasculate the political maneuverings these situations frequently create.

When focus is under threat. I don't know of two more formidable enemies of focus than prosperity and chaos. Both prosperity, blowing seductively in the organization's ear, and chaos, screaming epithets at the organization's gate, make it hard to pay attention. At the moment, I consider prosperity to be the biggest threat to the school I lead. It can undermine the urgency of our workforce while it tries to convince me that I can go ahead and concentrate on tasks other than the ones that helped create the prosperity.

Chaos, or what seem to be catastrophic problems, can also attack a leader's focus. I'm on the board of an organization that found itself in disarray. Its environment had changed, and the organization had not. We hired a new president who strolled into the situation with a positive attitude, a scalpel, and an admittedly authoritarian style. His first task was to listen to what everyone had to say. Next, he clarified the focus of the organization. Having completed those two steps, he passed out marching orders and pink slips. Focus returned, and the organization is in good shape.

I'm sure my objectivity is suspect in examining the authoritarian style of leadership. I don't particularly like it, and I wouldn't be very good at it. But I do believe certain situations call for it, and perhaps we are reaching one of those cultural situations. I won't be completely shocked if the authoritarian style makes a big comeback in the twenty-first century. As relativism seeps into every pore of our society, we will long for strong voices. Neither businesses nor individual lives will draw much direction from "I said 'maybe,' and I mean it!" Should this resurgence of authority-based leadership occur, we will undoubtedly face a different set of threats than those created by current distributed authority styles.

It will be interesting to see what form the authoritarianism takes, as well as how people react to it. But one thing I promise: The new authoritarians won't get away with offers to provide total direction in exchange for all of the freedoms that have been given in recent years. Nobody will make that trade.

DEMOCRATIC LEADERSHIP

I heard a story, perhaps a fable, about one of Carl Sandburg's final public appearances. Back in his hometown of Galesburg, Illinois, Sandburg ended a speech at Knox College to deafening applause and shouts of "Encore!" He shuffled back on stage and whispered, "Everybody is smarter than anybody," then departed. That, it seems to me, is the basis of democratic leadership.

Democratic leadership wears many faces and is perceived in many ways. Fans of the style venerate participative leadership by chanting, "people matter most." Cynics of democratic leadership deride it as "the animals running the zoo." Personally, I have found that my decisions usually improve when I get input from those who will be affected. Sometimes the substance of the perspectives strengthens the decision; other times, the process of discussing the decision helps me clarify its dimensions. The occasion is very rare when I'm not thankful I involved other people in making a significant decision.

Defining a democratic style can be slippery, but it is crucial to understand what it means to lead democratically. Leadership theorists from the 1950s to the present distinguish between a consultative process and a joint process. Yukl defines the former as one in which "the manager asks other people for their opinions and ideas, then makes the decision alone after seriously considering their suggestions." A joint decision, he observes, is one where "the manager meets with others to discuss the problem and make a decision together; the manager has no more influence over the final decision than any other participant" (2005, 157). This distinction is somewhat limiting because it forces "joint process" to mean one in which majority rules. A more important differentiation for me is the one between a democratic style and a democratic outcome.

Several years ago, our commencement exercises outgrew the venue that had been used for years. Either the impact of enlarged, blended families or the skyrocketing awareness of just how much fun can be found in two hours and forty-five minutes of pomp and circumstance fattened our attendance to an unmanageable number. At a president's cabinet meeting we boiled our options down to two alternatives. With no clear majority position emerging, we decided to poll ourselves. The outcome was five to four in favor of option one. I was in the "four" group, but pretty sure that option two was the way to go. So, in what was an unusual act for me, I smiled and announced, "The 'fours' have it." Everyone laughed, we chatted about it more to make certain we could all live with option two, and then we moved on to the next agenda item.

This example represents a situation in which the process was democratic, even if the outcome was not. Perhaps the style would have been more democratic if I had announced the "fives" had it. But the process was very participatory, and either way, I am held accountable for the outcome of the decision, whether I consult or join.

Incidentally, two weeks later, the cabinet members returned to report that the next level of the democratic process overwhelmingly supported option one, and that if I knew what was good for me, I would, too. "The 'fives' have it," I proclaimed boldly, and we were spared a bad decision. Clearly, the masses had outperformed the president on this one.

BENEFITS OF A DEMOCRATIC STYLE

Consonance. In America, rah-rah attitudes toward a "democratic" anything have not been restricted to the post–World War II era. This is the land of the free. We elect our leaders, and then throw the bums out if they flex their muscles a few too many times. We limit the powers of our president. We, the people, govern ourselves. So we can start with the premise that our democratic society has rubbed off on the general corporate culture of American organizations. Most workers will feel a certain consonance with a democratic leadership style. Even as a little boy listening to "Sixteen Tons," I shuttered at the totalitarianism implicit in Tennessee Ernie Ford's rueful groan, "I sold my soul to the company store." Having a voice lives in American hearts as an inalienable right—losing it when we join a group feels somewhere between disempowering and unjust.

Trust. The idealizing of democratic styles in the field of leadership was propelled by McGregor's famed "theory X, theory Y" proposition (McGregor 1960). Theory X leaders assumed workers to be disinclined toward hard work and require some form of external incentive to accomplish their tasks. Theory Y leaders assumed that workers possessed an inner drive to be productive that could be unlocked through trust and support.

McGregor may or may not have hit the target on what motivates a particular leadership orientation, but he was right about one thing: trust works. After a severe case of occupational aimlessness prompted me to drop out of Princeton Seminary, I went to work in downtown Chicago. My dad, who also worked in the city, rode a train that I could catch if I left work fifteen minutes early. After a few days on the job, I mustered up the courage to ask my boss if I could slide out before quitting time.

He responded by saying, "sure, your hours are 'produce.'" Two waves of his trust washed over me in that one statement. He trusted my integrity, and he trusted my competence. I did not disappoint him.

Good morale. A significant number of studies (though not all) cite findings supporting the belief that morale is higher in groups led by democratic leaders than in those led by authoritarian types (Bass 1990, 426). Certainly to the extent that democratic leadership builds on and communicates trust, morale will rise. But there are other morale-building outcomes of this style. In basketball, telegraphing a pass hurts the team. It allows the defender to anticipate. In organizations, telegraphing a pass almost always helps the team. It allows coworkers to prepare. In most organizations, morale is inversely related to the number of surprises. A democratically led environment necessarily engages people in the goals, directions, and strategies of the organization in ways that lift both anticipation and morale.

Improved decisions. It drives me crazy when a stealth cold call sneaks its way to my phone, and a salesperson asks me to consider buying some office item. Other than batteries for my Dictaphone, I can't think of one equipment purchase in which I would have adequate information to make the decision. I rely on coworkers to inform me on almost every decision I make. Leaders need good information. A democratic culture encourages the free flow of information better than the top-down slopes. Something very insidious can happen to leaders when they move into positions of authority. Generally, people gain positions of responsibility because they make good decisions. Once in the positions, these same people run the risk of thinking decisions are good because they make them. I'm a huge believer in instinct, but instincts with information hit the target more times than naked intuition. Democracies arm leaders with better information than autocracies.

Improved problem solving. Research in the field of group dynamics presents evidence that on non-complex problems individuals outperform groups (Shaw 1981, 60-1). On complex problems, groups do better than individuals. It's axiomatic that looking at a complex problem from many perspectives will result in deeper understanding and more potential solutions than can be seen from any single vantage point. Democracies, by definition, multiply the perspectives on the issues brought before the people. Generally, complex problems beg for the breadth only a group can bring. In complex business environments, democracies have the upper hand on autocracies.

Support. Back in the good old days, clever and loyal employees would scheme ways to plant an idea in the boss's head, knowing that implementation depended on him or her coming up with the idea. How the world has changed. Now the boss dangles ideas in front of the employees, hoping they'll take the bait and "own" the idea, knowing implementation depends upon them. Regardless of who engages whom, the odds of putting wheels on an idea rise when the implementers participate in the decision-making process. I have a friend who became a college president. He had perfected a style I would characterize as "leading by proclamation." I think he felt participatory decision making cluttered his genius. All it took was a couple of bad unilateral decisions, and the faculty handed him his lunch while the trustees showed him the door.

Clearly, implementation support rises when group members participate in the idea stage. Even if the deal goes sideways, the diffusion of ownership affords the leader some support born out of a "we're in this together" attitude.

DISADVANTAGES OF A DEMOCRATIC STYLE

Futility. An assignment given to me by our board of trustees takes the possibility of true democracy out of my hands. If my board chair asked, for example, "Bill, what were you thinking when you decided to allow alcohol in the dorms?" and I say, "I got out-voted," I'm history. The board has declared me a majority. So when I champion a democratic process that turns in a direction I can't support, I am immediately accused of staging a charade.

"Why bother asking us if you're not going to take our advice?" is a question I have heard on more than one occasion. My democratic pattern of getting input creates frustration when I have to make a decision that runs counter to popular opinion. What folks don't always understand is their input invariably improves my decision, even if it's not the one they would have made. Having said that, I find it both morally and strategically wrong to ask for advice if I have already made a decision. It's never right to fake democracy. When leaders employ "consulting" as a ruse for "selling" in order to get buy-in, they don't deserve to be trusted.

Pace. For three years in the early 1980s, I developed and sold cohort-based curricula to colleges and universities around the country. After being invited by institutions to make a proposal, I did market analyses, met with presidents, talked to deans and faculties, and then made my proposals. I'll never forget the first Catholic college I visited.

In the initial meeting, I met with the president and chief financial officer. When I asked them about meeting with all the other groups on campus, they told me, "Don't bother." So I never did. These two guys made all the decisions. I don't know if their authority had anything to do with the school being Catholic, but the power of the president felt papal in comparison to most colleges. It was by far the fastest contract I ever put together.

Without question, the whole program, both curriculum and contract, would have been improved through a democratic process, but it would have added a year to the process. Evidently, the two decision makers didn't feel they could afford the time that a more democratic style would have required. Democratic processes produce good outcomes, but they don't win many ribbons for speed.

Campaigning. Democratic leadership encourages two types of campaigning. First, people attempt to exercise horizontal influence, believing their potential for vertical influence gains strength with numbers. Communication networks go into high gear when an issue is in play. Gathering allies gets rewarded when group members can influence the outcome of a decision. Campaigning consumes organizational energy and threatens productivity, especially when the lines are lit up over ancillary issues.

A second kind of campaigning sometimes contaminates the democratic process. When every issue becomes a mule to carry forward some person's or department's imperishable agenda, it's hard to get a true read on the issue at hand. In some cases, these recurrent campaigns are both noble and work related, but they bias the process by inserting secondary concerns. Other times, issues are examined through the lens of some personal agenda. The purpose of an organization is to meet a designated set of mutual needs, not to provide platforms for our favorite "isms."

Inviting. The democratic style of leadership issues invitations indiscriminately. I sometimes brag to myself about how approachable people find me. I also sometimes loathe myself for maintaining an image that invites people to advise me on everything from soup to nuts. (Lest you think me cliché, I have in my possession a complaint about the soup in our dining commons, and I have another note observing that one of our erstwhile employees was "nuts.") The democratically oriented leaders implicitly welcome people to weigh in on all issues, not just the ones they place on the ballot. But you can't stand in the midst of your people and proclaim with great passion, "I want your input, but not on the stuff where I don't want your input." For a democratic leader, every day is the second Tuesday in November.

CONDITIONS THAT FAVOR DEMOCRATIC LEADERSHIP

When productivity depends on creativity. During 1985–86 I worked as a full-time consultant to the president of DeVry, Incorporated. In the for-profit sector, DeVry held the top spot in college-level technical training, largely through establishing the quality of its products and the well-being of its people as its highest corporate values. Phil Clement, the president, had no peer when it came to engaging employees. His leadership style was extraordinarily democratic in process, although far more consultative than acquiescent when it came time for a decision. Phil never failed to till those with information or perspectives related to significant decisions, but neither do I remember him concluding a discussion with, "Well, y'all, let's take a vote."

When DeVry's research team reported that we had pretty much penetrated our target markets, Phil knew that growth depended on innovation. We needed to supercharge the corporate culture with premiums for creativity. Phil launched an innovation campaign within the organization that culminated in a daylong process at the local Hyatt Hotel. We virtually closed the corporate offices and brought every employee into creativity capsules that spun off ideas as fast as they could be recorded. Phil facilitated the whole day himself. He embodied the value DeVry placed on the ideas of its people. Phil's stubborn demand that company leaders listen to the workforce paid off when several hundred employees gave him their best thinking because they knew it mattered. Phil Clement believed that everybody is more creative than anybody, and his democratic style helped the "everybody" to believe that as well.

When decision making depends on group members' information and support. I suppose this is a rather self-evident claim, but flashes of paternalism can draw leaders into a "father knows best" mentality, when father doesn't know squat compared to the rest of the family. Some decisions beg for group member participation.

Gary Yukl provides an excellent summary of the "information-acceptance" conditions that call for democratic decision making: (1) when the decision is important and subordinates possess relevant information lacked by the leader; (2) when the decision problem is unstructured and the leader does not possess the necessary information and expertise to make a good decision; (3) when decision acceptance is important and subordinates are unlikely to accept an autocratic decision; (4) when decision acceptance is important and subordinates are likely to disagree among themselves about the best solution to an important problem; and (5) when decision quality is not important but acceptance is critical and unlikely to result from an autocratic decision (Yukl 2005, 165).

I wish I had thought about these conditions before making the most important decisions of the first year in my presidential career. After a very careful analysis, I calculated exactly the way our organization needed to downsize. Unfortunately, this high-quality decision of mine got trampled when it hit the ground. My massive process error wasn't so much an act of autocracy as it was of being democratic with the wrong group. I conferred with the division leaders, but I left out the department heads whose acceptance was critical to the implementation. The substance of the decision was on target, but I'm lucky I survived the mess I made of the process.

When internal motivation is needed for productivity. Motivation for people to affiliate with groups grows out of some combination of two rewards: instrumental and intrinsic rewards. "Instrumental rewards" refers to the capacity for the group to act as an instrument in achieving a person's goals. "Intrinsic rewards" refers to the pure fulfillment that comes from being a part of the group.

Two of our children illustrate the difference well. Soon after graduating from college, our freshly degreed oldest daughter conducted a job search. She has a heart the size of Wisconsin and was looking to join a church staff where she could serve people, God, and strays of all species. She had a few great opportunities, but passed them by until she found the one satisfying her principal criterion: being appreciated and mentored by the pastor. Our college-sophomore son also looked for a summer job. He, too, had one criterion—cash. He would remove asbestos from nuclear waste containers if the price were right. Group hugs didn't rank too high on this kid's list.

People who participate in groups largely for intrinsic reasons need leaders who will engage them. These people value inclusion, the kind of inclusion that democratic styles of leadership create.

When group member stakes are high. Shortly after I arrived at Whitworth we decided to make a change in our benefits program. It was a no-brainer. We were adding choices to the plan. High fives from all the employees would be their salute of appreciation. Wrong. We got a few gestures, but none of them would be on your list of ways to express appreciation. I now have a new rule: If you're going to mess with people's health care, retirement, or anything else that might affect their quality and length of life, check with them.

Most of us are involved in organizational situations in which the individual's well-being is affected by the success of the whole. Democratic leadership allows the people to shape decisions and adapt to their outcomes as a part of the process. Conversely, folks who get broadsided by top-down decrees affecting their well-being will not be very good sports when the sycophants say, "Leader knows best."

The autocratic-democratic leadership style continuum provides a very useful perspective for leaders to use in checking their operating relationships. Although some situations benefit from an authoritarian leadership style, the balance of research tips in the direction of democratic leadership being the more effective style in the twenty-first century. This prediction, however, is qualified by many other variables, one being the leader's attitude toward tasks and relationships.

THE TASK-RELATIONSHIP CONTINUUM

As I mentioned earlier, I squirm a bit when I see "task/result" and "relationship" orientations on the ends of a continuum. They are not polar opposites. A leader could demonstrate both orientations or neither. For this reason I do not identify the benefits and liabilities of these two orientations in the same manner in which I present the autocratic/democratic continuum. In practice, leaders move back and forth between task- and relations-orientations more easily than they do between autocratic and democratic styles. In the known world's most comprehensive compilation of leadership studies, *Handbook of Leadership*, even Bass entitles the chapter on these studies, "Task- *versus* [italics mine] Relations-Oriented Leadership" (Bass 1990). The only lower case word in the title, "versus," reveals the way most researchers look at the relationship between these two variables.

In my simple definition of the task-relations continuum I put "what the group is doing" at one pole and "what the group is feeling" at the other. Task-oriented leaders place great value on completing the task. Relations-oriented leaders place great value on how group members feel about the experience. It is important, however, to bear in mind the difference between "orientation" and "effectiveness." We avoid socially oriented people who are socially inept, and we reassign, or eventually fire, task-oriented people who lack the skills to accomplish their tasks. Task- and relations-orientations refer to leaders' predominant concerns, not to their skill levels.

TASK-ORIENTED LEADERSHIP

One of my most memorable educational lowlights took place after a class in which my professor tested us to determine our task-relationship orientation. As a graduate student taking my first course in group dynamics, I had the blessing of studying with Em Griffin, a great human being and author of the best undergraduate communication textbook on the planet. After scoring our tests and explaining the orientation, Em asked us our scores. Well, he might as well have handed me a whip. I scored obnoxiously more task-oriented than anyone else in the class. So I tackled him after class. "Sorry, Em," I protested. "Your little test got me all wrong. I am very relationship-oriented."

Em, wanting to lighten my mood, smiled and said, "Maybe you just *wish* you were more relations-oriented."

"No, Em, I really am just the opposite of what this test says," I insisted.

Em chortled some lighthearted remark trying to get me to relax, but I was on a mission. I thought to myself, "Listen, Mr. Chips, you should see me in action. I'm so stinking relationship-oriented that people can't stop smiling for a week after they've had a load of me." So I came back after him a third time, but he stopped me

"Freeze!" he said. "Let's look at our exchange here. All I want to do is have a little relational fun with you, but you just can't let go of your task to convince me that you're not task-oriented. Think about it."

I've been thinking about it ever since.

Task-orientation in the leadership literature refers to the extent to which the leader is concerned with achieving the group's goals. Although task-orientation has been found in some studies to correlate with authoritarianism, theory X assumptions, and psychological distance from group members, such cold-hearted characteristics are not necessarily attributes of task-oriented leaders. These folks don't eat their young; they just want to get the job done.

My dear late mother's productivity drive bordered on the maniacal. Metaphorical to the way she lived her life was the one and only time my sister asked Mom to babysit her infant daughter, my parents' first grandchild. When the new parents arrived home at midnight, there sat Mom, reaching across the conked-out baby in her lap, banging away furiously on her typewriter. The new parents weren't sure if the baby had fallen asleep or just passed out from the sheer exhaustion of an evening with Grandma and her sacred to-do list. For people like Lillian Robinson, the addiction of getting things done makes geysers out of their adrenaline glands. Granted, Mom set the task-orientation bar a bit high for the rest of humanity, and she did leave a bit of social debris in her wake, but she made mincemeat out of those to-do lists. Task-oriented leaders will confess to the rush they get from finishing their jobs.

Most studies between 1950 and 1975 found task-oriented leaders outperforming relations-oriented leaders in the area of productivity. Even human-relations champion Renis Likert reported that a survey of several thousand workers indicated a tendency for productivity to be higher in the presence of increased pressure by supervisors for production (Bass 1990, 482). In some groups, task-oriented leaders received higher evaluations from subordinates than relations-oriented leaders, but undoubtedly other variables influenced the assessments.

Few enterprises will prove successful without any task-oriented leaders. Frankly, I know of none. But task-orientation darkens when it becomes "task-obsession." Today's quarter-to-quarter business cycle, combined with escalating competition levels in all industries, has created enormous pressure on leaders to keep moving the needle. These conditions leave us task-driven folks swimming dangerously close to some nasty whirlpools. Regrettably, I am an expert on these waters.

Blake and Mouton support the idea that leaders can be both task- and relations-oriented (1964). In fact, when tested for these orientations, I scored moderately high on relations—to go along with my perfect score on task-orientation. The tyranny of the task drive, however, often whips people like me back and forth between frustration and insensitivity. When tending to relations, I'm frustrated about burning energy on something other than our goals. So, then I get back in the task saddle and gallop past relational difficulties without even seeing them.

I'm sure different task-oriented people express their relational insensitivities in different ways. My way is shameful. I ignore the needs of the people closest to me. Apparently, when I'm bingeing on task, whatever energy I have left for relations I use on the folks "out there." I'm more likely to brush off my assistant, family, or the vice-presidents than the students or employees-at-large. In a perverse kind of way, I count on the inner circle to understand. When the task is completed, my sensitivity returns and I realize that I've been less than caring for the people I care about most.

The best way to tame our task-induced frustration and insensitivity is by: (a) redefining all tasks to include relational goals and (b) structuring interpersonal work into the task timelines. In other words, I've started trying not to abandon my task-related efforts in favor of relational work; doing so generates too much frustration. Rather, I'm reconstituting the way I think about tasks and the way I go about doing tasks to include components of relational productivity.

REFLECTION
HONEYMOONS

I've been on three honeymoons, so to speak: one with my wife and two as I've entered college presidencies. I botched the first two before having a pretty good third one. That there is a honeymoon is no fable; that the honeymoon involves a bracket of grace is no fable; but that the honeymoon offers amnesty from lasting consequences couldn't be farther from the truth. New leaders of colleges, and most other organizations, should think of their honeymoons as a short season in which the volume on everything they do is turned up full blast, with echoes that will be audible deep into their tenures. Unfortunately, most of us scream into the microphone. We want to show everyone it's a new day. All that junk we heard about the last president certainly won't be said of us, and we have just the right symbols to prove it.

My advice to new leaders is to think about the honeymoon as a time to be attentive and reserved, and not to be making too many style statements.

For me, learning this lesson was two parts failure and one part fluke. On our 1974 honeymoon with my wife, I wasn't attentive. On the honeymoon in my first presidency, I wasn't reserved. And I probably would have blown the third honeymoon were it not for a circumstantial quirk. When I came into my current position, two factors were very different from the first time around. First, I was the fourth president (including interims) since 1986, compared to being the fourth president since 1911 in my first appointment. Second, I followed an interim president whom virtually everyone on campus hoped would become permanent (after meeting him I agreed). So I started this job somewhere between cautiously and sheepishly. Compared to my first experience, I didn't sense enormous enthusiasm for either me or for the office I was newly occupying. But I had confidence in both my experience and in bright people who loved their school and would cheer for its well-being.

I learned two lessons that are probably applicable to most organizational honeymoons. I discovered that simply being new and in charge gave my words and actions all the amplitude they needed. When I attended a few student and faculty events, I was given honeymoon credit, actually more credit than I deserved. I didn't need to be ubiquitous to be appreciated. The other happy lesson I learned was that my restraint was helping to build a reasonable foundation of expectations and hopes for the years that would follow.

Research conducted by Estela Bensimon and Robert Birnbaum, eminent researchers of college presidencies, reveals that faculty members expressing disappointment in their presidents frequently cite a loss of the president's early attentiveness and enthusiasm (1992). I guess all of this is to suggest that new organizational heads should repeatedly think about the question, "What kind of foundation and patterns am I developing?" As leaders, we have the obligation of a consistent tenure in both form and substance. The artificiality of our honeymoon makes it a time when we are vulnerable to excesses that can threaten the durability of our effectiveness and ultimately hollow our leadership. But I must admit, even at partial throttle, honeymoons are still fun.

RELATIONSHIP-ORIENTED LEADERSHIP

Ways of describing relations-orientation that surface in the leadership literature include "relations-centered," "concerned with people," "facilitative," "supportive," and "interactive" (Bass 1990, 473). As I noted earlier, a relations-oriented leader is one concerned with how members are feeling about their whole experience in the group. For these leaders, it is not enough simply to complete the task.

When I interviewed our director of human resources for the job she now holds, I said to her, "Your job is to help make Whitworth College (now Whitworth University) a place where people love to come to work." We laugh about that rather vague job description, but we both know what it means. When people feel supported and valued, they live happier lives and do better work. I consider it both morally responsible and professionally smart for leaders to pay attention to the organization's human relations. Even the most task-oriented employee or group member longs for some measure of social support.

For the most part, experiments over the past fifty years provide evidence that job satisfaction rises in the presence of relations-oriented leadership. Specifically, a relations-orientation correlated positively with idea generation, group member self evaluation, role clarity, communication, morale, and performance on tasks (Bass 1990, 510). These findings come as no surprise. We all belong to groups that exist to accomplish something beyond just being a group. Intuitively, we know that when the group gets along well, more is accomplished and members are happier.

An implicit benefit found in the results of these studies is the motivational impact leaders create when they care about members' issues not directly related to the task. While working on my doctorate, I enjoyed the tutelage of a professor who allowed me to be his friend. Much of our relationship extended beyond our tasks as student and professor. I recall writing papers that I felt had reached the "A" level, and had met my standards, but they were never done until I could picture my teacher telling me what a great job I'd done. At work here was the principle of reciprocity. As my leader went beyond what was required for me, I went beyond what was required for my leader. This circularity showed me one of the most important principles of leadership I will ever learn: *Leaders get what they give.*

Possibly the greatest benefit that relations-oriented leaders provide their groups is putting themselves in positions to identify and remove impediments to productivity. In the early 1980s, I conducted roughly twenty market analyses in different cities around the country. My purpose was to determine area business-training needs. In each analysis I would poll managers and human-resources officers in various companies on the most salient problems in their workforces. For every technical problem reported, I'm sure I heard fifty human-relations problems. A relations-oriented leader can often see and address these difficulties before they throttle group productivity.

Freud built his psychoanalytic theory around the principle that, one way or another, we will communicate what howls within us. In the absence of a normal outlet, an abnormal channel will be used. It might be aberrant behavior, illness (psychosomia), tantrums, or some other form of attention-getting communication. The relations-oriented leader creates healthy ways to deal with the stress, ambiguity, and tension that can occur naturally in a work group. The removal of these barriers enriches the members and boosts their productivity.

There are, however, risks in overvaluing relationships. For three years, I reported to a very relations-oriented president. I loved just crossing paths with him in the hallway. He would whisk me into his office and pepper me with questions about my family, my job, and life in general. His generous spirit spread throughout the group who reported to him. Further, I felt his relations-orientation supported rather than supplanted his equally strong task-orientation. I'm not sure if the relational style of my charismatic boss caused me a loss of vision or a loss of nerve, but I didn't challenge him several times when, in retrospect, I should have. I didn't want to see flaws in someone who cared so deeply for me. At the time, I wasn't even sure if they were flaws. In the long run, he and I were both hurt by my silence; and I'm certain the organization suffered collateral damage as well.

Relations-oriented leaders believe rightly that their style opens lines of communication. However, they have to work very intentionally to tease out the concerns of their people. I know I could have spoken up, but usually I didn't and I never wanted to. He didn't need it, I thought. Exacerbating the problem, he wore his job pressures on his sleeve. So his countenance said "Talk to me," while the arm encased by the "job pressure" sleeve pushed away anything that might add to his load.

The ability to send this particular mixed message rubbed off on me. Even when I'm feeling particularly relations-oriented I should put a sign on my door that says, "Ignore my efforts to look busy and come right in, because I really do care about what you have to say."

Groups led by relations-oriented leaders can have a difficult time identifying and reporting problems, especially those caused in some way by the leaders. The groups must be provided with opportunities that invite expressions of concern.

Another danger faced by relations-oriented leaders poses a special threat in groups or organizations where the leader does not have direct contact with all group members. In Section I, I made the argument that most twenty-first century organizations will be geographically dispersed. By virtue of proximity, some people enjoy more time with the leader than others. It comes naturally to relational leaders to form close relationships with the people they encounter frequently. In the eyes of some, this creates a relational unevenness that smacks of favoritism.

Perhaps some leaders possess the emotional discipline to prevent frequency of contact from deepening a relationship, but that doesn't change people's perceptions of the inner circle, and holding the high-contact people at bay runs against the grain of relations-oriented leaders. More than with some dangers, this is one where being forewarned is being forearmed. Taking every opportunity to connect beyond the natural contact group helps even the balance of relationships. Because I do have friends and sports cronies with whom I work, I'm especially vulnerable to the "favorites" criticism. So I spend more time than many supervisors doing relational wandering around. And, actually, that also helps me better understand my tasks.

LEADING FROM THE MIDDLE

In this chapter, I've presented what leadership scholars have identified as the two most elemental styles and two basic orientations. All four of these categories are nourished by close proximity to the people being led.

Authoritarian. Leaders who function with an authoritarian style, whether because of their situation or their personality, need the middle. Because they have not heard the cheers and protests that rise from a democratic process, it is imperative that they be in a position to see how their decisions affect the people charged with implementing these decisions.

In my judgment, no United States president has blended authoritarianism and the middle better than Harry Truman. This man disdained (and often cursed) the pedestal. He stood among the American people and virtually said, "This is who I am. You decide if you want to elect me, but I will call the shots." He was legendary for calling the shots, and he was legendary for standing in the middle. After he left the presidency and visited what is now the Truman Presidential Museum and Library, he was known to give tours, answer the phone, and simply show up among the people. Harry Truman didn't convene too many focus groups to get advice or commission too many entourages to impress people. He stood in the middle and gave orders. Whether we loved or hated his decisions, being authoritarian from the middle was the essence of President Harry S. Truman.

Democratic. For the most part, democratic leaders are quite fond of the middle. But it's easy to get drawn away by other demands. The primary threat I see to the democratic leader drifting away from the middle is when the decision-making process becomes a substitute for listening to people. The vulnerability is found more frequently in large organizations than in small, one-shop enterprises. Leaders in these situations generally rely on representatives of the people rather than the populous itself.

For example, I am quite taken with how democratic I feel after asking the members of my cabinet to help me make a big institutional decision. I can very easily get lulled in to thinking I have my fingers on the pulse of the organization because I got nine different perspectives on my decision. But if I'm smart, I'll walk out of the cabinet meeting and head for the Union building to chat with students, faculty, and staff about issues surrounding the decision.

For any number of reasons, the members of my cabinet can give input that does not represent the perspectives of the people they represent. If I'm smart, I'll make sure I know that, regardless of the decision we end up making.

Task-orientation. Task-oriented leaders desperately need the middle. When task-oriented leaders get distracted from their groups' relational needs, leading from the middle offers a time-released antidote to their tunnel vision. In the throes of breakneck task pursuits, a very important question for task-oriented leaders to ask themselves is: "How will this hit the ground?" Drilling hard on the task can deafen a leader to warnings from the people. No one will ever know for sure whether Enron's Kenneth Lay was driven by greed or by love for his company, but he wasn't paying attention to his people. He didn't hear or he didn't heed the now-famous warning memo by Sharon Watkins. If Lay walked among his employees, listening to their hopes and dreams and commitments, would he have been willing to risk their futures? Would he have heard the warnings? Maybe it's generous to say that accomplishing the task (or some task) led to the blindness of the past decade's corporate crooks. But for some leaders, tasks can become taskmasters, and only the vision and the voices of the people can restore the kind of proportionality that leads to long-term success.

Relationship-orientation. Relations-oriented leaders often get caught in cross currents. Meeting the challenges of their tasks pulls them in one direction while their affinity for doing social maintenance carries them in another. These people need the middle in order to work from their strengths. Even for relational leaders, the task current is strong and can sweep them away from contact with behind-the-scenes group members. Dwelling among the people puts these leaders in a position to satisfy their relational inclinations with the whole group. You can't tend to group members' feelings and relations by remote control. I've tried it, and I've failed. When relations-oriented leaders lose touch with the people, they lose valuable "I care" chips and efforts to reconnect ring hollow.

It's all right for leadership scholars to identify a relations-orientation as a style, but caring for others as simply a strategy doesn't sell with the rank and file. For them, leaders must demonstrate the substance of authentic concern in attending to group-member relations. Intermittent grins and backslaps don't cut it. The middle of the group guides, fine tunes, and even corrects the leaders whose care they have learned to appreciate.

REFLECTION
THE CREDIT BOOMERANG

The first few years after my father retired from a twenty-nine-year stint overseeing a program he founded, it seemed to me he was neglected by those who carried on his work. He probably wasn't, and the sudden removal of attention didn't seem to faze him. This was the man who had so little ego that when he went to the event in which the 1974 Moody Bible Institute alumnus of the year was being announced and described, he whispered to my mother, "It's amazing how much this guy has in common with me."

To which she incredulously replied, "Paul, it *is* you."

I'll never forget Dad's confused expression as I looked over my mother's shoulder and realized that he was the only one of the twenty-five-hundred people present who was still in suspense.

When I entered the presidency, I followed a man who, like my father, had done his job well for thirty years, and remembering my father, I took every opportunity to tell the world what a fine job my predecessor had done. I vowed to myself that even at the risk of people bemoaning his departure, I would honor his leadership. What I discovered was that exalting his effectiveness did nothing to diminish people's perception of my own. Credit is not a finite entity that is exhaustible when distributed. It gains energy and magnitude when freely given. Leaders need to keep themselves in a salutary frame of mind.

I have learned this credit lesson well, but I still fail, more often than not, to practice it. My egoless father taught us repeatedly that we could accomplish much if we didn't care about receiving credit, and he was right. But I'm afraid I have taken the lesson a step too far—acting as though credit shouldn't matter to anyone. At times, I find myself agreeing with Pericles, who was reluctant to eulogize fallen warriors, believing their accomplishments should not be judged on the basis of how well he praised them. The big difference between Pericles and me is that the people I work with aren't dead and need to feel appreciated, whether I think praise is important or not. In this respect, the Golden Rule sometimes lets people like me down and should be rewritten to read, "Do unto others as they would have you do unto them."

I suspect that when I fail to notice the need to give praise, it is my ideal self rather than my real self that is shrugging off the importance of credit. We all need to be appreciated for our efforts.

Chapter Ten

Situational Influence on Leadership Style

I remember an interesting "leadership" day. At seven forty-five AM, I met with the whole staff of the university. Six times a year, we meet for thirty minutes to get caught up with each other. At noon, I chaired a meeting with twelve corporate CEOs and the presidents of four other universities. At three thirty PM, I met with the president's cabinet, consisting of the people who report to me.

In the first group, my position as president held significance in my efforts to inspire and inform the people. In the second group I was simply the facilitator, with my job getting me nothing beyond a seat at the table. On one side of me sat the president of a large land-grant research university, and next to him sat the majority owner of a publicly traded hotel chain. Neither of those two guys moved to the edge of their seats when the Whitworth president spoke. In the third meeting with my cabinet, being president held intermittent significance. I served roles as supervisor, group member, listener, informer, and occasionally president, as we discussed the operations of the institution.

Situation theorists believe these three different meetings called for three different leadership styles. What they call "situational moderators" influence the effectiveness of different approaches. For example, if we look only at my task- and relations-orientation in these meetings, the different leadership needs become clear. In the first meeting, I need to lead from a warm, relationship-oriented base. The task of communicating information ranks behind how we feel about one another. In the second meeting, both relations and task emphases are needed. I possess no authority as leader in this volunteer group, so a strong relations-orientation is required to make folks feel good about their participation. But it is never long before I feel the need to get very task-oriented in order to get things done. The conviviality of the group belies their demand that we achieve. The third group needs my task-orientation after a short time of social and spiritual renewal. We meet weekly, we like each other, and we don't like wasting time, but we're all smart alecks and we have a tendency to horse around while dealing with the agenda—except for our own agenda items. So, I need to be intermittently task-oriented without messing up the group chemistry we all enjoy.

Before reviewing the most significant ways that style and situation relate to each other, I want to comment on four ways of thinking about the adaptability of a person's leadership style. All four philosophies have been suggested, both implicitly and explicitly, by various leadership theorists over the past fifty years.

ADAPTABILITY THEORIES

Different leaders do well in different situations. This "different horses for different courses" approach rests on the assumption that leaders possess a dominant style. Matching these preferred styles with the situations that call for them results in a good leadership environment.

Leaders can be taught to adapt to the situation. Theorists holding this position believe situations shift too frequently to keep changing leaders. Leaders should learn to adjust their styles and emphases. Shifting lines every two minutes works better in playing hockey than in leading groups.

Strong leaders will change the situation to suit their strengths. My elementary-school gym teacher was an ex-Marine. We did nothing but march in three of our five weekly classes. I didn't stop liking it until fifth grade when I found out we were the only school in America with pre-pubescent battalions snapping to attention after fifty-five minutes of synchronized walking. To the four year old with a hammer, the world becomes a nail. In like manner, some leaders with a dominant, well-honed style see every situation as one that needs just what they have to offer.

Situations create leadership styles. This philosophy combines the first two and is held more often by historians than by leadership theorists. Proponents of this approach would defend the styles of Gerald Ford and Jimmy Carter as products of the post-Nixon era. The national political climate created by Nixon shaped the leadership styles of Ford and Carter.

In Section I, I discussed the need for paradoxical leadership, a style that demands adaptability. As a behavioral scientist, I believe internal and external forces sculpt a leadership pre-disposition in all of us. Transformational leadership, which has captured the interests of late twentieth century theorists (see Chapter Twelve), places its faith in the ability of leaders to be adaptive. In presenting the contingency models of situational leadership, I assume that leaders can alter their approaches. If nothing else, they can lean into the wind of their inclinations. Leaders predisposed toward task should build group relations prompts into their agendas. If their natural tilt is toward group relations, they should force themselves to focus on tasks.

FIEDLER'S CONTINGENCY MODEL OF LEADERSHIP

No leadership model has generated more research than Fred Fiedler's contingency model (Bass 1990, 494). As one of the first theorists to examine the relationship between style and situation, Fiedler ignited an interest that dominated the field for almost twenty-five years. I find it very interesting that in spite of Fiedler's profound influence, he is one of the only leadership theorists of his era to believe that leadership styles are somewhat intractable. His first choice for creating effective leadership would be to find the leader with the style needed for the situation (approach one, above). If that couldn't happen, Fiedler would advise the leader to try changing the situation. He believed that leaders could change situations more easily than they could change their own styles.

The contingency model of leadership looks at style in terms of task versus relationship orientation. I use "versus" advisedly. Fiedler didn't think the leader could be high in both. I, and many of his colleagues, disagree; however, I haven't seen too many leaders in whom one of these two orientations doesn't predominate. "Situation," in this model, referred to the favorability of the conditions. Fiedler defined very favorable conditions as ones in which a) the leader and group members had a good relationship, b) the task was clear, and c) the leader had positional authority. The most unfavorable conditions existed when none of those elements was present (Fiedler 1967).

I first studied Fiedler's findings in 1975. In virtually every leadership situation since, I have found myself "checking with Fred" to size up what is needed. Fiedler discovered:

- In extremely favorable conditions, a task-oriented leader proves more effective in accomplishing the work.

- In moderate conditions, the relations-oriented leader does better.

- In very unfavorable conditions, the task-oriented leader will be the more effective leader.

Fiedler breaks down the conditions very specifically and reports different findings for different combinations of the three situation components. In my use of his findings, I have simplified his analysis. I ask myself the following sequence of questions in attempting to size up the situation in groups I am assigned to lead:

What is the reason for this group's existence? Answering this question helps me to answer the second question.

What expectations does the group have of my role? I need to consider what the group wants from my leadership.

What is our task? I wrap goal, objective, strategy, and tactic differentiations into a general measure of task clarity. By establishing a sense of "task-readiness," I can avoid wasting energy on ambiguous task dead-ends.

What is the condition of the group? Again, I'm trying to determine a readiness factor. Either too little or too much time spent on relations can impede group progress. On this point I would add one factor to Fiedler's "situation favorability" conditions. Earlier, I made the distinction between instrumental and intrinsic reasons for joining a group. Some folks join only for what the group produces, while others might participate largely for the affiliation. It's helpful to know members' motivations and expectations.

Is this group a rocket waiting to be launched or a sack of parts waiting to be assembled? In other words, is this a really good or a really bad situation? I know that my task-orientation lends itself to very good and very bad situations. Under such conditions, I don't need to spend too much time talking to myself. I can engage in a little social gesturing, drop a load of hurry on the group, and we're off. Under moderate conditions, I find it helpful to think of myself in the dual role of human-relations coordinator and task champion.

THREE SITUATIONAL VARIABLES

I feel the interaction between a person's leadership approach and the favorability of the situation represents a very influential variable affecting leadership effectiveness. Fiedler suggests trying to change everything but the leader's orientation when remediating a tough situation. I disagree with Fiedler. We hold greater access to our own behaviors and attitudes than to those of the group. Further, shuffling leaders around to fit situations works well in experimental settings, but in real life we often need to work with the hands we're dealt.

Fiedler identified three variables that determined the favorability of a situation:

- **Leader-member relations:** the degree to which the employees accept the leader.

- **Task structure:** the degree of task structure and the clarity of the goal.

- **Position power:** the authority the leader possesses by virtue of his or her position in the organization.

The three situational variables that I find most compelling borrow heavily from Fiedler, but they are broader. In suggesting them, I have drawn from at least a half-dozen contingency theories and decision models, as well as from my own experience. Some situational theorists present elegant typologies that predict twists and turns with greater specificity than I find realistic. But sensitivity to the presence and influence of these situational factors will serve leaders well to the extent they can adapt their dominant styles.

Perceived power of the leader. I do not believe that "leader position power" (Fiedler 1967) or "the authority given by the organization" is as important as the power followers give to their leader. Young Life, Inc., an interdenominational ministry to junior-high and high-school students, pounds the mandate into every one of its staff members that "You have to win the kids every day." In that same respect, I believe leadership power is won more than assigned. Few would argue that as long as group members have a choice, only they can grant a leader the power to influence. But do leaders really operate on the assumption that their followers are their most important source of power?

A leader approaches every situation with different kinds of power. Since the studies of French and Raven (1959), the nature and degree of power in groups has captivated the attention of behavioral scientists. French and Raven's power bases include:

- *Expert power:* group members' perception of the leader's competence.

- *Referent power:* group members' identification with or general fondness of the leader.

- *Reward power:* group members' perception of the leader's ability to provide rewards.

- *Coercive power:* group members' perception of the leader's ability to evoke punishment.

- *Legitimate power:* group members' belief that the leader has the right to lead (also referred to as "positional power").

Three other types of power that I have seen offered in various forms:

- *Information power:* group members' perception that the leader has valuable information.

- *Goodwill power:* group members' perception that the leader cares about their well-being.

- *Short-straw power:* group members' assignment of leader status without any basis other than that they need someone in the role.

The fundamental question leaders should ask themselves in assessing the conditions of every leadership situation is, "Why me? What do the group members feel I bring to this situation that will prompt them to accept my leadership?" The answer to this question inevitably draws upon several power bases. If we fail to ask the question, or to answer it correctly, the following problems may result:

Assuming the wrong base. On occasion, academic deans will discover academic department chairs assuming levels of expert power and legitimate power when other members of the department are granting little more than short-straw power. These chairs must *earn* perceptions of expertise and legitimacy if they hope to function in any role beyond coordinator.

Squandering a base. The first capital-campaign consultant I retained after I became a college president drove me crazy. Supposedly, this person's reservoir of experience formed a strong base of expertise. Yet her mode of operation was to finesse out of us what we wanted to do, and then slap our hand if we failed to meet the timeline. We granted this person a truckload of expert power, but getting substantive advice out of her bordered on the impossible. She did little more than keep us on schedule.

Depleting a base. This problem occurs when we fail to recognize that our power almost always emerges from an arrangement of bases, rather than from one exclusively. For example, giving orders without explanation can allow our bases of expertise and information power to atrophy while exhausting our referent or legitimate power. Parents exploit their coercion power when they bark to their children, "Because I say so!" C'mon, Dad, tap into a few other bases. Nobody wants on their epitaph, "His strong suit was coercion."

Ignoring a base. Everybody feels the love when a leader claims that true power is granted by the followers, but it can cause the leader to under use positional power. I'm guilty of that. I explain, I inform, I charm, and I talk about the abundant rewards as I dance around various bases, inviting my cabinet to grant me power. I know I have ignored my legitimate base when, in the middle of one of these performances, someone says, "Bill, make a decision." Sometimes we fail to notice the power bases that can strengthen our leadership.

Perceptions people hold of their leaders' power exert huge influence over the leadership situation. Leaders must direct and moderate their styles depending on the nature and degree of their power. Too often we overlook the "Why me?" question.

Trend-line of the organization or group. Often leaders need to think in contrarian terms, especially when their organization finds itself in a steep upward or downward turn. I catch myself trying to influence our culture by sending messages that offset the messages being sent by our trend line.

I'm not sure that I ever consciously choose to alter my style on the basis of prosperity and morale, but I know that I do. I find myself attempting to supply what I fear the organization could lose. Hence, in the challenging times, I'm pretty upbeat. When prosperity returns, I have a tendency to work with a furrowed brow.

I have assumed the presidencies of two colleges in the midst of declining enrollments. In considering whether to accept the jobs at both institutions, I didn't really think the task of increasing enrollments would be all that formidable at either place. Both schools had good missions and strong histories. There were plenty of areas that scared me, but I felt pretty sure I knew which buttons to push for attracting and retaining students. My confidence, coupled with the prevailing fears of the faculty and staff, prompted me to exude optimism. I served not only as president, but also as cheerleader and soothsayer. I wanted folks to know that our great mission and great people were a "can't miss" combination.

As enrollment fortunes reversed in both situations, so did my emphases. I became more task-oriented and less rah-rah. I worked harder. We had all hustled like mad to turn things around, and I didn't want a sense of complacency to undermine our progress. Inspiring hope when things looked discouraging and providing urgency when the future looked rosy represented efforts to supply what I didn't want the colleges to lose.

I learned about the importance of urgency in reacting to a trend line at Princeton Theological Seminary. My best friend there, Ken West, was a great tennis player who now writes wonderful books on parenting and human development. Ken would spot me thirteen points in a squash match, and then play me to fifteen. When I got good, he granted me only twelve points. During various sports, I noticed that when Ken got on some kind of a scoring streak (which was often), his already high intensity level would just shoot off the chart. It didn't even look like he was having fun. When I asked him what demon invaded his body when he got on a roll, he gave me an answer I've never forgotten. In essence he told me the fiercest enemy of momentum is momentum. When you get it going, everything feels easy; none of the voices within you push you to work harder. In other words, momentum breeds a complacency you must battle with all of your energy. Momentum is what we work to achieve, and it requires almost more work to keep it than to get it.

At a conference of college presidents, a group of us discussed the vanishing breed of long-tenured presidents. We concluded that it is still possible for one person, but not one "presidency," to serve effectively over the long haul. In other words, a leader must make fundamental adjustments in style and emphasis for the group (the college, in this case) to stay relevant and fresh. As conditions change, the leader must adapt. Both the organization and the leader will benefit.

Psychological needs of the group members. My observations about trend-lines apply primarily to entire organizations. In considering psychological needs, I'm referring to individuals and small groups—particularly to the leaders' immediate working groups. On a grand scale, I provide leadership for Whitworth University, but to get that done, I give direct leadership to the ten people who report to me. It is this group whose psychological needs I must consider in calculating adaptations I need to make to my leadership style.

Any discussion of the interaction between leadership style and psychological frameworks must include Paul Hersey and Ken Blanchard's Situational Leadership Model (1969). The Hersey-Blanchard model attempts to match the best leadership behavior with the maturity level of the group members. Their hypotheses are more applicable to the superior-subordinate relationship in an organization than to volunteer-based groups.

A good bit of controversy swirls around the Situational Leadership Model. Bass observes, "The Hersey-Blanchard model has had remarkably widespread intuitive appeal to practicing managers and to leaders of management training programs, despite its theoretical inadequacies and the paucity of supportive empirical evidence" (1990, 492). Criticisms notwithstanding, situational leadership has become one of the most enduring management tools of the twentieth century. The essence of the theory can be briefly summarized:

- Managers are most effective when they are able to diagnose their subordinates' "willingness" (attitude or confidence) and their ability to perform the task before them. There are four readiness levels of followers and four associated management styles based on these readiness levels:

Readiness Level One: low ability and low willingness. *Leadership style:* telling.

Readiness Level Two: low ability and high willingness. *Leadership style:* coaching or selling.

Readiness Level Three: high ability and low willingness. *Leadership style:* participation or encouragement.

Readiness Level Four: high ability and high willingness. *Leadership style*: delegation.

- In general, psychologically immature groups and group members benefit most from a strong task orientation. Mature groups and group members benefit most from a strong relations orientation.

- The most effective leaders possess both high task- and relations-orientations and adjust their style to the maturity levels of those being led.

I believe that the best way for us to adapt our styles to a person's psychological needs is to take a run through my altered version of the

Golden Rule: *Do unto others as they would like you to do unto them.* This rule provides an antidote for judging other people's needs on the basis of our own (closer to the real Golden Rule, but not as effective).

When I was an academic dean, an assistant dean reported to me. I had not chosen him; he was a gift, as it were, from my provost. I thought this colleague had a bit of an ego when he pouted to me about how devastated he felt over my failure to introduce him properly to a group of faculty members. I didn't overhaul the style with which I dealt with him until the day he bounded into my office and asked if he could trade his new salary increase for the more gallant title of "associate" dean. "Sure," I bubbled, and a happier, albeit poorer, associate dean left my office. We got along better when I understood his values and needs.

We can make very helpful style adjustments to provide psychological support to the folks for whom we provide leadership. It requires attentiveness to notice their needs, compassion to provide for those needs, and humility to keep ourselves from thinking they should have different needs—ours, for example. Without being duplicitous or loosening their integrity, good leaders treat different people differently. That's part of the art of leadership, but we must also know our own psychological limits. I'm wretched with tender egos. I'm not as bad as I was when I shamelessly let that associate dean give back his raise, but I'm still not very good.

To adjust our styles to other folks' needs, we need to understand our own. For some people we don't have an adjustment in our kit that will work. We can't lead them and we shouldn't try. A change in groups by at least one of us offers the best bet for both to be happy. But for everyone else, our ability to lead will rest on sensitivity to their needs and our capacity to adjust our style appropriately.

Former U. S. Senator from Oregon Mark Hatfield once said his biggest challenge as an elected official was discerning when to lead those who put him in office and when to represent those who put him in office. Most members of Congress will find that one approach comes more naturally than the other. In some respects, the leader of the group or organization looks at similar choices and has corresponded pre-dispositions. When should leading be leader-centered and when should it be group-centered?

Leadership studies suggest that leaders carry natural inclinations toward authoritarian or democratic leadership into their organizations. Evidence also supports the claim that organizational situations shape the style of their leaders. It is safe to say that the majority of the studies conclude that, in general, a democratic leadership style out-performed an authoritarian style in areas of group-member satisfaction and productivity (as measured in the long run). But exceptions to this general finding abounded, as some groups, depending on the situation, experienced better results under authoritarian leadership.

During the middle of the twentieth century, most theorists believed that leaders' tendencies surfaced in styles that matched better with some organizational situations than others. As we consider recent trends in leadership theory, matching leaders' styles with the right situations will give way to the philosophy that good leaders bend their leadership orientations in order to adapt to the changing needs of an organization. The trend will absolutely blast its way in to the twenty-first century.

Leading from the Middle

I am plagued, and occasionally blessed, by many off-campus involvements. Most of them hold strategic potential for advancing the university, but valuable or not, they take me away. When I am not traveling, family and civic duties crowd my schedule. I serve on a lot of boards, and, more importantly, I serve as a husband and as a father to my children.

All of these duties compete with my efforts to lead from the middle. Much of the time, I'm not anywhere near the borders of our school. I have realized that all of these external duties make barging my way into the middle of our people more important than ever. It has become very clear to me that the less time I spend in the midst of the people and programs of Whitworth, the more programmed my leadership style becomes. Conversely, I find myself far more adaptive when I'm moving among our people. I don't know if distance causes me to lose my sensitivity or my confidence or both. Maybe the piles of accumulated work that greet my return force me into a rigid get-it-done style. Whatever the reasons, I know the middle makes me more nimble and adaptable.

Several weeks ago, I met with three people who wield a lot of influence over my schedule. Going into that meeting, it was important for me to have a clear sense of which events brought me into the nexus of our university life. But some years, I'm just gone. This past year, I fell well below my average on time spent in the middle. Receding campus involvement triggered my leadership default settings, and my style became stiffly task oriented. If I hope to avoid a repeat of last year, I must know the most efficient paths to the middle, then elbow my way past the opportunities that attempt to pull me off the paths.

Chapter Eleven

Transformational Leadership

The final era of the twentieth century was one in which the potential to exercise leadership reached every member in every corner of the organization. The authoritarian leaders of centralized organizations in 1900 would not recognize the distribution of leadership that represents the twenty-first century ideal. One hundred years ago, who would have imagined that the most venerated leadership expert in America would suggest leaders establish a relationship of "mutual stimulation and elevation that converts followers into leaders and may convert leaders into moral agents" (McGregor 1960, 4)?

A soccer coach nicknamed Thor used to coach for our school. To label Thor as stoic would be like characterizing the Pacific Ocean as wet. Thor's bench style was inert. When the match reached a fever pitch, we would watch Thor for any signs of what physicians call "a pulse." When Thor lowered his brow, we would all speculate what might be causing his temper tantrum. To say the least, Thor was understated. But, oh, how his boys could play soccer. "Spirited" is a mild euphemism for their furious intensity. And they seldom lost.

The trait theorists would have had to spend an entire season in Thor's back pocket to find the personal attributes that made him a great coach. But his basis for his success becomes much clearer when Thor is seen through the prism of transformational leadership. By the time matches began, Thor had skillfully transferred his leadership to the men on the field. Followers had been transformed into leaders, working toward a common goal worthy of demoting any individual objectives. Thor exerted what we call a transforming influence over his team, in spite of his frozen demeanor.

It's easier to point to Thor's influence than to come up with the definition of transformational leadership. Actually, there is no one, agreed-upon, definition. We shouldn't be surprised; with as much trouble as scholars have agreeing on a definition for leadership, the odds are slim that adding the rather slippery adjective "transformational" will clear things up. Fortunately, the term carries enough properties common to all definitions for us to get a pretty good idea of what it means. Starting with the ideas of several experts in transformational leadership will help us surround, if not define, the term:

James McGregor Burns. Not to confuse a Scot with a Spaniard, but Burns is the Picasso of leadership thought. His 1978 work represented a different way to think about the art of leadership, and virtually all leadership studies since have been influenced by his work. Burns says transforming leadership is a "relationship of mutual stimulation and elevation that converts followers into leaders and may convert leaders into moral agents" (Burns 1978, 4). He continues, saying transforming leadership is "evolving interrelationships in which leaders are continuously evoking motivational responses from followers and modifying their behavior as they meet responsiveness or resistance, in a ceaseless process of flow and counterflow" (440). Burns's notion of leadership focuses on mutuality, process, and adaptation. Burns also campaigned harder for the moral dimensions of leadership than most theorists who went before him.

Bernard Bass. Yukl summarizes well Bass's notion of transformational leadership: "The extent to which a leader is transformational is measured primarily in terms of the leader's effect on followers. Followers of a transformational leader feel trust, admiration, loyalty and respect toward the leader, and they are motivated to do more than they originally expected to do." These leaders elevate the importance of the task, inspire followers to put the group interests before their own, and "activate their higher-order needs" (Yukl 2005, 351).

Bass built on the work of Burns, and many theorists believe the outcomes of Burns's transforming leadership parallel those of Bass's transformational leadership, even though the definitions differ. The big difference between Burns and Bass lies in the nature of motivation. Where Burns heralded morality as essential to transforming leadership, Bass stresses nobility.

Gary Yukl. I like Yukl's clarity in most everything he writes. He defines transformational leadership simply as "the process of building commitment to the organization's objectives and empowering followers to accomplish these objectives" (2005, 350). Yukl comes closes to the kind of leadership found in the "Level Five" leaders that Jim Collins found in great companies—"it's not about the leader."

The succinctness of this definition sounds quite close to antecedent theories. But Yukl's cornerstones of "process," "commitment," and "empowerment" still support the foundation of transformational leadership. Style and situational theorists would consider these elements superfluous to the leadership needed in some situations.

CHARACTERISTICS OF TRANSFORMATIONAL LEADERSHIP

Based on my studies, experiences, and efforts, I have come to believe that transformational leadership relies on three characteristics that are necessary but, admittedly, not sufficient. I am not suggesting these three elements are all one needs to be a transformational leader. In fact, I am assuming the pre-existence of a basic leadership capacity. But I have come to believe the presence of these dimensions is what differentiates transforming leadership from the trait-based or style-based models. In order to meet the requirements of Burns's lofty definition, transforming leadership must be authentic, adaptive, and interactive. Remove any one of the three, and Burns's description crumbles.

Authentic: In 1991, I found myself seated in front of the presidential search committee at a prestigious non-sectarian university. This meeting concluded three days of preening around campus as one of two finalists for the job of running the school. Amidst all the fanfare, both my wife and I felt disquieted over the fuzziness of the mission and way in which several faculty members brandished their "open-mindedness" as they raised concerns that I might be influenced by my faith. So I was feeling a bit confused and agitated when the search committee concluded our three days by asking me if I'd seen anything I didn't like about their university.

This question triggered what became my leadership moment of truth. I replied, "Yes. Your mission statement is built around the claim that you 'search for excellence, wherever it may be found.' I'm not sure what that means. Frankly, I haven't been able to figure out the soul of this university."

Without knowing it at the time, I was really talking to myself as much as to them. That experience awakened me to a bright awareness that my image of being a leader placed an *authentic commitment to mission* squarely in the middle of the picture. In other words, my understanding of a leader was of a "transforming" leader.

You can't fake transformational leadership. I do not believe leaders can boost followers to transcendent levels just by going through the right motions. I think transformational leaders must be absolutely sold on the mission of their organizations. I admit in one respect, transformational leadership reaches back to the situational models. Leaders must be selective in choosing to lead only in groups and situations where they can provide authentic enthusiasm for the mission. It's at this point I accept the distinction between managing operations and leading change. A good manager can be effective in far more situations than a transformational leader can. Good management requires delivering the right style for the operational demands of the situation. I don't think transformation occurs unless a leader brings to the organization or group a deep belief in the fundamental importance of the mission. Without that conviction, efforts to bring group members to higher moral planes, or to inspire them to put the group needs in front of their individual needs, will ring hollow.

When I received a call about Whitworth, it was from the same headhunter who'd led the presidential search in which I couldn't seem to find the soul of the institution. He claimed to have the perfect school for me. On paper, Whitworth had two strikes against it. First, the institution was in a bit of a bad mood. Several years of struggle over enrollments and finances had stirred the faculty and contributed to the prior president's decision to leave suddenly. I had enjoyed enough success in my short career to allow me to select my way around that kind of a deal. Second, Whitworth presented itself as a Christian college. Though firmly committed to the Christian faith, I believed that colleges could not huddle behind any wall of orthodoxy and claim academic authenticity.

At many Christian colleges, hard questions posed as threats rather than as sharpening stones. That made no sense to me. As an educator, I believe truth is quite muscular. It doesn't need our protection, and if God's word is true, it should be able to take on all comers. By faith, I believe when we stand with truth, we stand with God. We must pursue truth, whether in the cynical halls of our disciplines or in the hostile alleys of our culture. I doubted I could be faithful to my professional convictions in a Christian college.

So as I considered Whitworth, I battled a bias. Most liberal arts colleges I knew were either suspicious of faith in their reverence of open-mindedness, or they frowned on open-mindedness in their protective attitudes toward faith. In choosing between the two imbalances, I had come to the conclusion that I would fare better as a defender of faith in a more liberal academic environment than as a defender of openness in a narrow Christian college climate. A good liberal arts college needs a word from both Jesus and Bertrand Russell, and I decided I'd rather be where I was stumping for Jesus.

But as I looked at Whitworth, I was intrigued by what I thought I was seeing. The school seemed different from either of my two models. Somehow God's providence, deft leadership by the board, or dumb luck had endowed Whitworth with a fierce embrace of both Christian conviction and intellectual curiosity. I was astonished. I asked friends at Christian colleges what they thought about Whitworth. I loved it when I heard, "They're pretty liberal; they can't decide whether to be Christian or secular." Friends at secular schools also gave the right answer: "Great school, but very conservative; they can't decide who they want to be." The fact that Whitworth was Presbyterian, as were Bonnie and I, put whipped cream on the situation.

When I arrived at Whitworth, my number-one priority was to find out if the people really understood and loved this rare alchemy of conviction and curiosity. All the problems and opportunities could wait. I had moved a long way and passed on some pretty good situations primarily for a mission. I needed to confirm my hope that it was the real deal.

What I discovered thrilled me. The Whitworth community embodied this distinctive mission, but they weren't really aware of its gemstone value and didn't do a very good job of naming it. I had walked into a situation that was absolutely ripe for me to take a shot at transforming the culture. The components were fail proof. First, the mission overlapped significantly with my deepest personal and professional values—I would never tire of promoting it. Second, this mission provided a very uncrowded market niche. Our faith emphasis put us on the right edge of secular institutions and even most church-related schools, while our fervent openness placed us on the left edge of Christian colleges. Third, Whitworth had underestimated its precious uniqueness.

My principal job as leader was to transform the way Whitworth College thought about itself, its mission, and its potential. The energy with which I tore into this task arose from my own deepest convictions. If I was nothing else, I was authentic in declaring the worthiness of the Whitworth mission.

In telling my story I risk giving the terribly false impression that I am quite noble, or that authenticity requires a mission of some glorious contribution to humankind. Neither is true. All I'm saying is that people in positions of authority have no chance of providing transformational leadership if they simply follow their noses to work every day, flip on the switch, say all the right things, then drag their fannies back home. As relief pitcher Tug McGraw chirped every time he opened his mouth during the fabled 1969 New York Mets march to and through the World Series, "Ya gotta believe."

I knew a guy in Pittsburgh who ran a company that made screen doors. You could not afford to ask him about those doors. If parents loved their children like he loved his metallic gates of splendor, it would be a better world. The man believed, and transformation can't take place without that kind of authentic leadership.

Authenticity is validated when people stand at close range. Observation is a greater power than overt persuasion. Said another way, a picture is worth a thousand words. When people see the depth of our convictions operating in everyday work, it turns up the volume on our claims. For me, leading from the middle accelerated the rate at which our people began to trust my efforts.

Adaptive. When Tom Matthews strode into Spokane, more than one of us had visions of a new sheriff. Donning a ready smile and wielding the reputation for a fast trigger finger, this Texan considered "business as usual" his number-one enemy. His new position as CEO of a big public utilities company put him in charge of the city's largest employer. With firmness and charm, Tom announced from day one that Washington Water Power, soon to take on the less regional name of Avista Corp., would adapt to the new economy or get eaten alive. Tom didn't much like the second option.

Transformational leaders all suffer from a touch of schizophrenia. Sometimes they respect history and deplore the present. They appreciate the efforts of their predecessors and they learn from the past, but they spit in the eye of the status quo. Other times, transforming leaders disdain history and relish the present. They bristle about their powerlessness over past performance but squeeze every drop out of the present. Regardless of which side of the past-present disorder you bump up against, you will not find a satisfied bone in their bodies. They're always ready to adapt, to change. Never quite transformed and always transforming, these leaders are absolutely intolerant of inertia.

It was interesting running across Tom Matthews during his first year on the job. He actually broke the schizophrenia mold by grousing about *both* the past and the present. The poor guy was in such a hurry to get to the future that everything seemed slow to him. He came out of the chute slashing the company's stock dividend by 61 percent while chasing down a few billion dollars in capital. He expanded operations into nonregulated, Internet-based markets and projected IPOs that he thought would spin back value to the shareholders.

Why was Tom in such a rush? Because he believed he was running a high-tech energy business, not a utility business. He knew that Avista could crank out profits for a few more quarters without major changes, but in this new world, the race to innovate was off and running. Tom had every intention of keeping his company, shareholders, and himself in that race. Company efforts turned toward fuel-cell R&D, fiber-optic networks, Internet-based billing and calculating, etc. Avista's employees joined Tom in thinking differently about the nature of the company.

Jack Burns observes, "Adaptive action is not the characteristics or traits of a leader… (it) requires leaders and followers to participate in a process" (1996, 156). Most Avista employees clearly bought in.

Unfortunately for Avista, the slope of its prosperity curve eventually turned sharply south, demonstrating the risk inherent in rapid adaptations. When Bill Gates picked up 5 percent of the company and Merrill Lynch analysts blessed it with a "strong buy" rating, Avista's stock volume exploded and its price tripled. Investors believed that "ol' Washington Water Power" had been transformed into an adaptive company, ready to parlay the next generation of high technology.

Well, they were wrong. Extraordinarily bad luck, and a couple of very bad decisions, ganged up to deliver Avista a big financial slam. Its stock price returned to the pre-Tom Matthews level, as the company was pummeled by astronomical year-2000 prices for the energy it had contracted to sell at a fraction of what it cost. When all this hit, Tom took responsibility. Although he could never have anticipated the skyrocketing price of energy, he was the leader, and bad stuff happened under his watch. Several Monday-morning quarterbacks agreed with him when he accepted full responsibility for the problems. Eventually, Tom Matthews resigned under fire.

Some blame his style, while others blame his substance. But his successor, Gary Ely, and number-two person, Scott Morris, will say straight up that much of what Tom Matthews did had to be done. My own opinion of Matthews' downfall is that he worked harder at adapting his company to the industry environment than adapting himself to the corporate and regional culture. He imposed his vision instead of extracting it from the strength of his people and the opportunities in the market for which Avista was uniquely prepared. Leaders must recognize that adapting their organizations to the environment works best when they adapt themselves to the organization's strengths and build support for change.

Being an adaptive leader doesn't always turn out rosy. It requires a stomach for risk, and as we learned from the technology companies that drowned in a wave of red ink in the first few years of this century, risk is risky. But the twenty-first century will demand moves and counter-moves by its leaders. Leaders will adapt or be gone—maybe both, depending on how they go about it. But all organizations will lose ground in rapidly changing environments if their leaders are slow to adapt. Perhaps more than ever, leaders who can engineer successful adaptations will be in huge demand.

Interactive. The leadership-theory folks seldom use the term "interactive" to describe the relationship between transformational leaders and the people they lead. "Mutual" or "shared" more frequently appear in reference to this tie. Generally, I would prefer an outcome term such as "mutual" to an input descriptor like "interactive." One could argue it doesn't matter how the leader and followers reach the point of feeling that "we're in this together," but when it comes to leadership, I think it does matter. Profit sharing, employee stock options, and employee ownership all build mutual benefit between management and employees, but they do not create transformations. People must feel engaged by more than structure. They need to feel a human connection. Six times each year, I begin the day with our staff for a time of "inspiration, update, and questions." I try to create a spontaneous, interactive feel to the meetings. Our human resources director believes those twenty-to-thirty-minute meetings, preceded by coffee and fellowship, have created higher levels of confidence and trust in the administration than anything else we do. Although they use vastly different styles and methods, transformational leaders never lose contact with their people.

Those of us who live in the Northwest spin great Bill Gates yarns. We all know Microsoft employees and erstwhile employees (a.k.a. millionaires) who worked with Gates. One of my favorite stories I heard from a friend who's also a friend of Gates's father. When young Bill came home for spring break during his sophomore year at Harvard, his father asked friend Sam to talk some sense into his college kid who wanted to drop out of school. Sam agreed and took Bill Jr. out to lunch. After their two-hour meal, they shook hands and parted company. Sam walked straight to a pay phone and called Bill's dad, "Hello, Bill," he said. "This kid doesn't need Harvard."

Whatever you believe about Microsoft, Windows, or Bill Gates, one thing you can know for certain: Bill Gates knows the Microsoft behemoth. In his days as its CEO, one way or another, he pumped blood to every corpuscle of that company. It could be claimed that no one in history has done more to accelerate and expand human contact than Bill Gates. That's no accident; I think he created Microsoft just to keep up with himself. I'm not sure whether the Internet provides a metaphor for Gates, or if it's the other way around. The guy gives new meaning to the word "connected."

I have a friend who recalls his first Bill Gates meeting as a Microsoft employee. Everyone knows that in your hour with the chairman, the sin for which there is no remission is that of being unprepared. The mind facile enough to wing it with Bill Gates waits to be discovered. My friend, who was one of several people in attendance but not presenting, left the meeting absolutely stunned at Gates's performance. Every question Gates asked was perfect as he surgically disassembled and rebuilt the issues. The presenter had spent weeks preparing for his hour as navigator of the complexities. His job was to keep the chairman from any unproductive paths. Inefficiency steals the attention that interactive leaders need to give to the next issue. My friend reported that the meeting ended with a $100-million decision.

The legendary interaction stories of Bill Gates set a ridiculously high bar, but they do make the point. Transformational leadership skates along the ridge between empowerment and engagement. Leaders who empower but don't engage come across as disinterested. They rob group members of the leader's big-picture view. It feels like they've gone golfing while everyone else works. On the other side of the ridge, leaders who engage but don't empower feel paternalistic and meddling. Genuine interest can get interpreted as checking up or as a lack of confidence. Skillful interaction allows the leader to learn and advise without invading the delegated responsibilities of the team members.

In my judgment, maintaining a healthy ask-advise equilibrium is the most important balancing apparatus in walking the ridge. Transformational leaders both proclaim and procure information throughout the organization. Leaders should enter meetings armed not only with information, but also with questions. The symbolic value of this practice is good, but it runs a distant second to the real insight leaders can gain from listening to employees' ideas. This balance between asking and proclaiming helps establish the sense of mutuality that can transform the culture from being upward and downward into forward. Moreover, as interaction transforms the organization, messages get communicated by the culture as much as by pronouncements from the leader. This is why I consider the transformational model of leadership to be more anthropological than economic. The former communicates through high ideals and norms, while the latter communicates through exchanges and deals. Transformational leaders savor interaction with those they lead.

CREATING CULTURE

Transformational leadership ripples through an organization. To quote Burns, "Transforming leadership converts followers into leaders" (1978, 4). Empowerment acts as the electrical current in this conversion. Group members' motivation and commitment rise in proportion to their responsibility. They become transformers in the distribution of organizational energy. Confidence and accountability recharge group members as they take ownership of the vision.

To look only at the formal leader in a transformation model is to misunderstand the fundamental nature of this approach. Transformational leadership shifts the spotlight from individuals to relationships. Leaders' roles change, and they ask new and different questions. "Was I clear enough with Megan for her to get the job done?" is replaced by, "Do Megan and I have the kind of relationship that gives her the confidence to attack the job but the security to ask freely for my advice?" Transformation takes place through building and equipping, not assigning. Leaders can't expect cartwheels from their people if the authority they distribute has a leash on it.

The most fundamental ingredient in the distribution of leadership is mutual trust. In the first two years of *Christianity Today*'s national survey on the attitudes of employees at Christian organizations, Whitworth ranked as best workplace in its category of colleges, universities, and seminaries (Lee 2003). Besides some good publicity, the reward for that ranking was a visit from Al Lopus, president of the Best Workplaces Institute, to review the results of the employee survey they had administered to participating organizations. He attributed the success of Whitworth and other healthy workplaces to "engaging its employees in an environment of trust." Leaders will empower only those they trust. Workers will accept empowerment only from those they trust. And I think the leader should make the first move. When Helen Lee interviewed me for a follow-up article in *Christianity Today*, she asked whether employees should have to earn our trust before we place our confidence in them. I think a better question is whether we should have to earn our employees' trust before they put their confidence in us.

Setting these kinds of climate conditions ranks as one of the most important jobs for the main leadership gardener. It's easier to do this with our immediate work groups than with the entire organization, but it's no more important. A study by Kozlowski and Doherty found a significant correlation between the quality of leader-subordinate relations and subjects' satisfaction with the organization's climate (1989).

Leaders need to think about what kind of culture will best nourish leadership within their organizations, then put together a plan for making it happen. E.H. Schein suggests five opportunities for leaders to shape culture (1992):

- Being selective about where they focus their attention.

- Asking themselves how their reactions to crises will affect the desired culture.

- Modeling the values they want to permeate the culture.

- Rewarding desired values and activities.

- Hiring and firing based on cultural expectations.

Each of these activities provides the leader with an opportunity to grow leadership throughout the organization. Too often we forget about the impact our decisions have on culture. I watched one of our vice presidents bring swift resolution to a stalled decision when I simply asked her what influence the retention or dismissal of an employee would have on the leadership culture within the institution.

Most leaders would benefit from mining the vast leadership resources buried within their ranks. Their organizations' leadership quotients would skyrocket if people looked at issues in terms of leading rather than simply executing. Those of us in the leader positions must provide rich soil for leadership to grow. Transformational leadership is distributed and pervasive. It is not a finite commodity. When used, inventories replenish themselves with increasingly higher levels of quality. Transformational leadership is judged not by looking at the leaders, but by the quality and extent of leadership exercised throughout the organization.

Leading from the Middle

One day, I took a break to run over and catch a swim meet on campus. Because this was a killer day work-wise, I had only about forty minutes to give, so I had to make it count. The main folks I wanted to see were the swimmers, not only in their events, but between the immersions that would surely drown most mortals. As I was dashing back home, I asked myself if darting into the middle for a short time did anything whatsoever to help our swim coach provide leadership. I didn't do much, but I did have the chance to mention how highly I regarded our coach's work to three of our swimmers and their families. And I hope being there even for a short time communicated my belief that this program is important. So maybe a few minutes in the middle helped our swim coach a little in providing leadership to all the people he touches. I hope so.

It may be wishful thinking to claim we make our people better leaders by rubbing shoulders with them now and then. An argument could probably be made that we have the potential to intimidate or divert leadership when we enter the domains of our people. But precious few of the folks we lead will claim we diminish their leadership effectiveness with our presence.

If leaders hope to transform a culture, they must be willing to enter and affirm the colonies led by the people from whom they desire leadership. They must embody their expectations. Being an exemplar is tough to delegate.

Transformational leaders in the twenty-first century will be the champions of progress because they are authentic, because they are willing and wise adapters, and because they maintain high levels of interaction when they lead. Public sentiment and, in extreme cases, government regulations will come down on the heads of manipulative leaders. The aftermath of the self-serving executive financial packages that contributed to the creation of Sarbanes-Oxley rules will be a society that demands authenticity from its leaders. When the 2008 economic crisis triggered the U.S. federal government's decision to enact the Troubled Assets Relief Program (TARP), common sense predicted that executives of massively failed banks would ratchet back their obscene compensation plans. Common sense was wrong, and the American public was outraged. Authentic leaders reflect the values of the organizations they lead. Amidst the tragedies of the global economic meltdown was the faint good news that scandalous leaders were exposed. Hopefully, this exposure will pave the way for authentic leaders who reflect and exalt the values of the organizations they lead.

SECTION SUMMARY

In this second section I have presented the most enduring findings of leadership theory's brief, hundred-year history. Somewhat arbitrarily, I have divided this history into four periods in which research focused on leadership traits, styles, situations, and transformation.

I offer two perspectives to the leader who desires to learn from this history. First, it is important to note that over the course of this century the general trend of leadership studies has shifted its focus from the leader to the followers. Early studies searched for the personal characteristics that made great leaders. Current thinking looks for leader*ship* throughout the organization. The growing complexity of today's enterprises forces a diffusion of leadership. Leaders must not only provide leadership, they must create and inspire it in others. No longer will single sources of expertise, direction, information, and power be able to satisfy adequately an organization's needs to be responsive to changing environments. In other words, it has gotten rough for leaders who try to go it alone.

The second perspective I urge in looking at leadership history is one of respect. Even though contemporary experts present quite different views of leadership effectiveness than early researchers, the discriminating student will realize that current theories build on rather than replace past findings. In everything ranging from meeting new people to guessing on multiple-choice exams, experience teaches us to trust our first impressions. I have presented historical theories as trustworthy first impressions of the field. I am suspicious of researchers who tout their findings as corrections of past errors. Their hubris sounds very tactical to me. Certainly, we have added much knowledge since the early days, but I encourage readers to learn from the durable insights found in leadership studies throughout the twentieth century.

SECTION III

CHANGING OUR BEHAVIOR

One Thursday night, a CEO friend of mine asked me what I was doing over the weekend. When I told him I was writing the last chapter of this book, he sighed, "The people who work for me love reading books on leadership, but I can't see where any of them are getting any better at leading anything."

Nobody has ever risen from being an ineffective leader to being an effective leader by reading a book on which steps to take. Frankly, that isn't about to happen to anyone racing to the last page of this book. Books don't change people. People change themselves through the decisions they make. Some great ideas about what changes we would like to make can be found in books, articles, speeches, counseling, and in a host of observations we make about the world around us. Personal growth is achieved through the discipline of our own decision making.

This last section is less about becoming a better leader than it is about how people make significant changes in their behavior. Since we can't become better leaders without changing our actions, this section is worth reading. It is also worth reading because the approach to change I'm suggesting can also help us change our behavior in every other area of life. I know this is big talk, but it works. I've seen it work with prison inmates, athletes, supervisors, and CEOs. I've seen it work in my own life.

Having claimed that this section is worth reading, I admit that it is also one you might want to skip. Its advice won't work unless you are willing to work, and work hard. I am certain this section has the formula for a huge step up in the leadership effectiveness of most people. I've seen it in myself, and I have seen it help others. Anyone willing to commit to each component of comprehensive change can expect significant results. But the commitment is serious.

CHAPTER TWELVE

THE THEORY OF CHANGE

Simply *wanting* to change isn't enough. It never has been. You might want to eat less, exercise more, lead more effectively, and play lead guitar for REO Speedwagon. But something happens between wanting and succeeding.

By my admittedly crude calculations, roughly 520 times between the ages of seven and seventeen I vowed on Sunday night that I would "be a better Christian this week." Simple vows would carry me through until mid-Monday morning. On those particular Sunday nights when I rededicated my life to God, I was a better Christian almost all day on Monday. If we had a special speaker *plus* I rededicated myself, my trend line didn't wilt until at least Wednesday. But I remember no Friday in which I could detect any residual effect of my Sunday night guilt, shame, and resolve. My weekly backslide became so regular that my attitude toward the Second Coming of Christ became "The earlier in the week, the better."

There's no doubt that my desire to be a good Christian was sincere, albeit transitory. In fact, I majored in religion and philosophy in college, eventually going on to seminary. During those years, my understanding of faith grew at a faster pace than my practice, but both improved. Yet it was not until I turned from my theological studies and delved into the behavioral sciences that I began to understand just how complex and multifaceted life changes can be. At the master's level I studied the process of persuasion quite intensely, discovering that the meaning, origin, and persistence of being persuaded varied greatly across people and circumstances. Although I became more intrigued with major life change, I was still pretty confused about where and when it would strike.

My first real understanding of change came during my last semester of doctoral classes at the University of Pittsburgh. I was enrolled in a social psychology research seminar where we studied attitude change. The text, by Martin Fishbein and Icek Ajzen, cited surprisingly discrepant findings in studies of the relationship between attitude change and behavioral change (1975). The authors explained these inconsistent outcomes as the result of imprecise definitions of "attitude" and ambitious leaps from measuring attitudes to predicting behavioral change. In reviewing hundreds of studies, they found researchers were defining any kind of predisposition toward an action as "attitude." Unless theorists looked at an entire group of these predispositions, they would find many unsupported hypotheses between an attitude and the behaviors they expected to follow. For example, during my "seven-to-seventeen years," a researcher could have asked me any of the following questions in search of my "attitude:"

- Do you think God is displeased when you use profanity?

- Do you think profanity is unbecoming to you?

- Do you like to use profanity to make a point?

- Do you ever feel good after using a bad word?

- Do you plan to stop using profanity?

- Are you intending not to say any bad words on Monday?

Some studies defined attitude so broadly that each of these six predispositions might have been used to represent my general attitude toward profanity. Not only was this an imprecise definition of attitude, it also required a hefty inference to jump from the answer to any one of these questions to predictions about me cleaning up my mouth.

Fishbein and Ajzen believed that a person's behavior was the product of an interaction among his or her beliefs, attitudes, and behavioral intentions (1975). Basically, they claimed that beliefs represent a person's information and convictions about an object or behavior. Attitude, as distinguished from the other two components, is how a person feels (likes or dislikes, for example) about an object or behavior. Intention refers to a person's plans to perform a particular behavior. Fishbein and Ajzen defined behavior as observable acts of the subject or person. In the profanity example, beliefs would refer to the first two questions (displeasing to God and unbecoming); attitude would refer to the second two questions (liking to use profanity to make a point and feeling good after using profanity); intentions would refer to the last two questions (not cussing on Monday and stopping altogether); and behavior would refer to acts related to profanity, such as cussing at friends, teachers, coaches and, of course, ministers.

In this example, Fishbein and Ajzen would confidently predict an end to my profanity if they found that I started believing it was bad, stopped enjoying it, and planned to stop using it. They would be less confident in their predictions if they knew that my intentions, for example, had changed and I planned to discontinue using profanity. Fishbein and Ajzen believed that because researchers frequently measured only one of these three components, they often found an equivocal relationship between attitude change and a corresponding change in behavior.

THE B-A-I-E-E-B MODEL

The following is my adapted version of the Fishbein-Azjen model, arranging what I believe are the dominant influences on behavior:

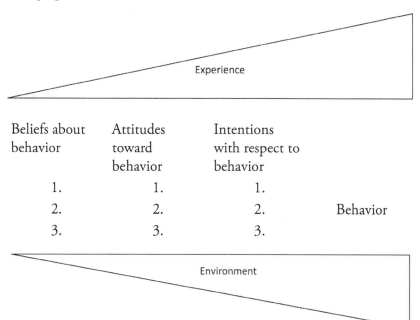

Beliefs about behavior	Attitudes toward behavior	Intentions with respect to behavior	
1.	1.	1.	
2.	2.	2.	Behavior
3.	3.	3.	

The angled lines encasing "Experience" and "Environment" symbolize the way in which the strength of these two influences grows as one moves toward the performance of a behavior. The well-known syndrome of what Irving Janis coined as groupthink (1972)—the reverence for unanimity—illustrates the power and progression of experience and environment over behavioral change.

Janis goes into significant detail on how groupthink infected President John F. Kennedy's inner circle. He cites Arthur Schlesinger Jr.'s reluctance, preceding the ill-fated Bay of Pigs invasion of Cuba, to voice dissent. The force of *environment* is clear in Schlesinger's lament, "I can only explain my failure to do more than raise a few timid questions by reporting that one's impulse to blow the whistle on this nonsense was simply undone by the circumstances of discussion" (Schlesinger 1965, 255). Further, Schlesinger's *experience* with expressing objections also discouraged him from dissent. He reports a private conversation in which Bobby Kennedy chided him, "You may be right or you may be wrong, but the President has made up his mind. Don't push it any further. Now is the time for everyone to help him all they can" (1965, 259). This self-censorship demonstrates how Schlesinger's past experience and the prevailing environment bore down to prevent a behavior that he *believed* was important, *felt* he should perform, and *intended* to do.

DEFINITION OF TERMS

Because the purpose of this discussion relates to major changes in behavior, these definitions make no attempt to define terms in their broad sense, but looks at them only as they relate to a particular behavior.

Beliefs: the information, knowledge and conclusions that we assume to be true about a behavior.

Attitudes: our feelings about a behavior; liking, disliking, feeling good or bad about the action.

Intentions: our plans with respect to a behavior.

Environment: the context in which a behavior occurs and in which intentions, attitudes, and beliefs are formed.

Experience: our past encounters with a behavior or issues and actions related to the behavior.

Based on theory and supported by my experience, I have come to believe that our behavior changes to the extent that our beliefs, attitudes, intentions, experience, and environment propel the change. Here is a simple example that puts these five components of change in context:

> While Larry was faking enthusiasm in his annual review, his boss was faking satisfaction with Larry's performance. Weary with the dance, Larry blurted, "What do I have to do to get promoted?"
>
> His boss quickly replied, "Show some leadership!" In the honest conversation that ensued, Larry discovered that both his boss and his coworkers felt that he had often personalized issues in a way that caused him

to be defensive and impaired his judgment. His boss reminded him how two weeks earlier she had told him that his department needed to come up with a plan to shorten the amount of time it took them to fill work orders for other departments. He became very upset. He proceeded to give her concrete instances of how delays were not the fault of his department. Now, Larry's boss was telling him that his pattern of reacting to suggestions and requests made her fearful of promoting him.

"How are you going to improve if you interpret requests and suggestions as attacks?" she asked. "Frankly, we're able to get away with very few improvements to your systems because you've become so good at compensating for the process flaws. But at the next level, we need someone who can look objectively at the big picture and make it better."

Larry proved his boss's point by arguing that she didn't understand his area, and left the meeting upset with her. Later, Larry felt remorseful. This was not the first time his defensiveness had gotten him in trouble and he knew it. Larry wished he could change.

There are many different ways for Larry to go about changing this pattern of defensive response. But he needs to deal with all five components that influence his behavior:

Beliefs. Larry's been watching too much football. He thinks the best offense is a good defense. He must *believe* suggestions and criticisms are opportunities to learn and to grow. He must *believe* not all calls for improvement are personal criticisms. Unless he has evidence to the contrary, he must *believe* people's motives can be trusted. He must *believe* problem solving will produce better results than defending. He must *believe* he holds greater security in being open to feedback than in protecting himself.

Attitudes. This is a tough area for Larry. He feels rather heroic when he rises to his department's defense. Larry didn't get an A in debate by cowering from a challenge. He feels good carving up an opponent.

Besides, Larry took a lifetime worth of crap from his "perfect" older brother; he doesn't need anymore from anybody else. But Larry needs *changed* feelings rather than *hurt* feelings. He needs to let himself enjoy the cooperative spirit of "Let's see if we can improve this." He needs to fear and repel the first signs of the defensive reactions that call him to combat. He needs to enjoy teamwork and welcome outsiders with suggestions as honorary team members. He needs a new *attitude* about feedback of any kind. He needs to love ideas for improvement.

Intentions. Larry is fun. He's spontaneous and loyal. He's a great friend to his friends. Unfortunately, spontaneity and loyalty conspire against Larry at work. Larry needs to get ready to change. He needs a *plan*. He needs to have clearly in mind how he will respond the next time he senses the first sign of criticism, feedback, or suggestions for improvement. He needs some kind of an alert that will remind him *not* to do next what comes naturally. Initially, Larry needs an intervening device that reinforces his commitment to bring his behavior in line with his beliefs. He needs a set of specific intentions to break his pattern of defensiveness.

Environment. Larry knows there are certain circumstances that flip his switch. He is also aware there are situations in which he has been generous in spirit. To whatever extent possible, Larry needs to engineer his *environment* so that he is responding in circumstances that support his desired behavior. Larry has discovered he benefits from a cooling-off period. Because situations affect him so strongly, Larry should make stalling a part of his new pattern of behavior. In fact, Larry might do well to suspend his goal of nondefensive behavior and replace it with the more modest goal of muzzling his first response. Perhaps, as he becomes less defensive through the use of cooling-off periods, he can back off somewhat on delay being his first reaction. There is no dishonor in using crutches to help effect change.

Experience. Early in his career, Larry was burned by a coworker whose advice he trusted. Since then, only the folks Larry knows well have been rewarded with his trust. This is where Larry should start. He should ask a reliable coworker, someone he can trust, for suggestions on how he could improve his work. This would allow Larry to prepare himself to respond, and he needs a few early wins.

Psychologists call this positive reinforcement. Larry can be forgiven for some caution in the early stages of his efforts to change. It is important that his new behavior of openness be rewarded with a successful experience. This is where Larry's boss must be attentive to his desire to change. She must make him feel successful and protected when he lowers his fists and works cooperatively toward improvement.

This little example touches on a few ways in which Larry can work on each of these causes of behavior. However, the process is more complex, and the causes run deeper than suggested by this quick fix for Larry. The following premises form the foundation of my system for changing behavior:

1. To change a pattern of behavior, one's beliefs, attitudes, intentions, experience, and environmental influences must work together to support the change.

2. Erratic behavior is the result of beliefs, attitudes, intentions, experience, and environmental influences moving in conflicting directions.

3. These components exercise influence over each other, sometimes in an overpowering way.

Not long ago, a discouraging report surfaced in which it was revealed that a group of teens, who had heard messages about the risks of smoking for several years, had picked up the habit at exactly the same rate as the control group that did not participate in the anti-smoking program. I wonder where the program sputtered. Perhaps the students *believed* all the health problems related to smoking were too far in the future to really matter. Or maybe the information wasn't convincing enough to overcome their "smoking is cool" *attitudes*. It could be that some kind of pledge not to smoke, similar to the kind of vow that some teenage sexual abstinence groups use, would have fortified their *intentions*. Perhaps when the students entered an *environment* in which the majority of students had not been indoctrinated, they just caved in to the social pressure. Or maybe these students had *experienced* homes and social circles where smoking was heartily approved. I'd love to read the researchers' assessment of why the program didn't work. I'd be willing to bet that a weakness could be found in at least one of these five areas.

As suggested in the "Larry" example, patterns of behavior change when all five of the components I've identified agree to work together (premise one). Occasionally, one or two components can out-muscle the others in the battle over behavior (premise three), but it's usually a group project that leads to significant change. For example, when I was thirty, a doctor told me I needed a healthier diet. What he said made sense to me (beliefs), and I really liked fruits and vegetables (attitudes). So, I was in good shape on beliefs and attitudes. However, Bonnie and I didn't change our shopping patterns (intentions), I wasn't a pound overweight (experience), and I ate better than most of my friends (environment). So my periods of healthy eating were sporadic, with my beliefs and attitudes pointing toward broccoli, and my intentions, experience, and environment pointing toward ice cream (premise two).

At age forty-five, I discovered my cholesterol was up, my friends were starting to eat more wisely, and my wife started buying healthier foods. When my experience (cholesterol), environment (friends), and intentions (food purchases) came in line with my beliefs and attitudes, my healthy eating became a pattern rather than an intermittent response to my internist's good advice.

As noted in premise three, sometimes one component can overpower the rest. I have a friend who learned after a checkup that his initial blood work had broken every cholesterol record in the Pacific Northwest. When he asked his doctor if they were going to put him on a treadmill, she gasped, "No!" and said he'd be lucky to make it to his car. Suddenly, his *attitude, intentions,* and *environment* yielded quickly to his *belief* that cholesterol causes heart attacks and to his new information that he was *experiencing* a small city's worth of the stuff sludging through his arteries.

Perhaps the most important lesson to be taken from the three premises is that the key to a life change is that there is no one key. Major behavioral changes require major changes in the causes of the behavior. As Fishbein and Ajzen discovered, you can't pull off change by working only on one area. Many times, I have responded to an article or speech on leadership with a new attitude or some new ideas, but seldom did I do the work necessary to change a pattern in the way I lead.

Unfortunately, we can't simply enter into a new understanding (beliefs) on how to be a better leader and assume we will therefore be one. We can't walk out of an inspirational management seminar pronouncing new excitement (attitudes) about being a good leader and assume we will therefore be one. We can't assume if we make up one of those beautiful personal-growth plans (intentions), complete with a mission, strategies, and tactics on being a better leader, we will therefore be one. Even if we have benefited enormously from the changes we have made (experience) and find ourselves working in situations that provide sufficient safety to make more changes (environment), the patterns of our leadership behavior won't change if we rely on only one of these factors to carry the load.

On the other hand, we *can* change if we are willing to work on each and all of the five causes of behavior. The good news is that (a) tackling each cause breaks down the process of change into manageable tasks, and (b) a new set of causes will have greater staying power than trying to discipline your self without much support beyond "wanna."

CHAPTER THIRTEEN

SIX STEPS TO SUCCESSFUL CHANGE

Julie Andrews was wrong. As much as I like *The Sound of Music*, the "Do Re Mi" tune gives bad advice. To "start at the very beginning" is *not* "a very good place to start." If we want to be better leaders, we need to start at the end result we're after, and then work our way back to "a good place to start." It won't work to begin with the question, "What beliefs do I need to be a better leader?"

The following steps suggest a process for making major changes in the way one leads. If it is followed, even the most stubborn behaviors can be reformed.

STEP ONE: SELF-ASSESSMENT

I have a friend who confided in me his concern that he's too quiet around coworkers. "I'm trying to draw them out, sort of invite them to participate by my silence," he explained. Well, you'd have to administer smelling salts to his coworkers if you were to suggest this guy is "too quiet." He's developed the harmonica effect of talking both while exhaling and inhaling.

It is not possible to achieve the right results with the wrong goal. We must know our strengths and weaknesses in each behavioral area we are trying to improve.

The ways in which we assess ourselves in a behavioral area differ little from the ways we assess an organization. Through a series of measures we identify perceptions of our strengths and weaknesses. Of course, ego plays a larger role in assessing ourselves than in assessing our organizations. It's risky to gather our colleagues' perceptions of our personal strengths and weaknesses and then compare them with our own. We might end up with a bigger list of weaknesses than we're prepared to see. But it is essential if we wish to complete a successful change in behavior. As I have argued, beliefs form the foundation of our behavior. Our efforts will eventually crumble if our foundation is built using bad information. The inaccurate self-assessment of my loquacious friend will lead to an ugly awakening if he puts together a program to become more talkative.

Unless a person suffers from a psychological disorder, the primary tools needed to do good self-assessment are *courage* and *honesty*. To be sure, some very helpful instruments are available that can give feedback about one's leadership strengths and weaknesses, but I find their usefulness limited for two reasons. First, most of these tests measure our proclivities and preferences more than our capabilities and actions. Second, they often force their users into generic boxes that are not custom made. I vote for the more primitive method of people sitting down with a legal pad and honestly recording what they feel are their strengths, weaknesses, likes, dislikes, accomplishments, and failures in a certain behavioral arena. Having dealt with themselves, they then need the courage to elicit feedback from people in a good position to provide evaluations in the same areas.

STEP TWO: GOAL-SETTING

Setting goals for changing a pattern of behavior is not the same as putting together performance goals for a MBO program. As it relates to leadership, goal setting for large behavioral changes is less scientific and more general. When someone pulls off a major change in the pattern of his or her leadership behavior, no one will need a calculator to verify the success. Changes of this magnitude are both self-evident and evident to others.

Good goals in changing a pattern of behavior should meet three requirements:

First, they must really be worth accomplishing. People who are willing to take on the big job of changing beliefs, attitudes, intentions, environment, and behavior will lose their traction if they discover the goal won't deliver what they're hoping for, or that it isn't worth the effort.

Second, our goals must be within the right attainability range. When we build too much stretch into our goals, we have an excuse to give up by blaming our surrender on unachievable goals. On the other hand, goals that are too modest won't sustain our efforts. The meager magnitude of change fails to keep us motivated. We need attainable goals, but ones that require significant effort. Some years ago I set for myself the goal of becoming a teaching president. In addition to all the duties attendant to being a college president, I committed to do research, get current in my discipline, and teach a course every semester. Midway through the first course I agreed to teach, I found myself resenting my professional first love—teaching. Even though I had bent my beliefs, attitudes, intentions, and environment into supporting this goal, I decided I would wait until I moved out of the presidency before I would teach another class. In retrospect, I wasn't changing my behavior as much as I was *adding* to it. My goal was too ambitious.

Third, our goals must be compatible with our basic genetic makeup. We can't change our DNA. When I announced five years ago to Bonnie that I was going to undergo a major personality change and become a safer, more conservative person, she laughed and said she'd be satisfied if I just stopped picking up unsavory-looking hitchhikers. Changing a pattern of behavior is different than becoming a different human being. We need to set goals within the limits of who we are and what we have been called to do.

Good goals are ones that matter and ones that can be attained.

STEP THREE: BUILDING BELIEFS

When I was in my early thirties, I found myself failing miserably at every effort to change certain things in my life. I had applied my B-A-I-E-E-B model, but it seemed to break down whenever it came time for the desired behavior. Finally, I reached the conclusion that I had some psychological defect, and I sought out a counselor. Although I'm sure I entered into counseling with a full complement of psychological disorders, my counselor startled me by suggesting my failure to achieve the changes I was after was not a psychological problem. He delivered the news after I sighed, "Look, I just want my behavior to correspond to what I believe I should be doing."

His response was, "It does. You don't really believe you need to change." He went on to suggest that I rather enjoyed the way I was acting and in my heart and mind I didn't really believe my actions were all that problematic.

I'm not sure whether my counselor was completely accurate in his assessment, but he did make a point that I've never forgotten. Our beliefs are potent influences on our behavior. Fishbein and Ajzen make the claim that "the totality of a person's beliefs serves as the informational base that ultimately determines his attitudes, intentions, and behaviors" (1975, 14). Although I do not agree that beliefs are as deterministic as this quote suggests, I do agree that they are the most powerful cause of the behaviors we choose. I find it a bit misleading to picture one's belief system as the *origin* of attitudes, intentions, and behaviors. If that were the case, we could focus exclusively on our information, knowledge, and convictions, and assume the rest of the causes would fall in line. For me, a better metaphor for the role beliefs play is that of a leader/supervisor, with attitudes, intentions, experiences, and environment all reporting to beliefs.

Using this image of beliefs as the leader or supervisor, we can categorize belief strength using various leadership typologies presented in Section II. I find the Tannenbaum and Schmidt's model works well in arranging the role and strengths of our various beliefs.

Teller beliefs. Our strongest beliefs, teller beliefs require all of the other causes of behavior to conform to their rule. For example, I believe intensely in the importance of leading with civility. It is a teller belief of mine and it battles any signs of insubordination from my attitudes, intentions, or environments. When I am unjustly accused and feel retributive, my attitude tries to get an exception from my belief in civility. Almost always, my civility belief will order my attitude back into shape.

Seller beliefs. Although these beliefs operate without significant alteration, they are not as strong as teller beliefs. I love watching two of my nonfaculty coworkers when their seller beliefs are in action. In particular, these guys maintain the seller belief that shared governance is a necessary part of higher education life. They have seen the value of faculty governance in academic matters, but I would not say that their belief in shared governance ranks up there with God and country, for example, as a teller belief. Their minds are always trying to sell their attitudes on the notion that they should be happy they don't have to mess around with all the academic issues. It's clear to me their intentions are obedient to this seller belief, as they ask faculty members questions and seek to understand academic processes. They also have enough belief strength to drag themselves into the prosaic environment of faculty meetings. Ultimately, their seller beliefs call the shots on shared governance, but these beliefs have to work hard to sell their convictions to their attitudes.

Consulter beliefs. This set of beliefs invites influence from attitudes, intentions, experience, environment, and even our actions, but ultimately it supervises the other causes of behavior. It is in this category that Leon Festinger made a hit with his theory of cognitive dissonance. Festinger, as well as other cognitive consistency theorists, claimed it was quite natural to minimize the dissonance between what we believe and the actions we take or the attitudes we hold. We feel pressure to bring our beliefs closer to our actions, or vice versa. Aesop demonstrated this point when his fox concluded that the unreachable grapes were sour anyway. Entire libraries have been filled with research studies and hypotheses on cognitive consistency and dissonance reduction. Virtually all of this research would agree that our tentatively held beliefs are more susceptible to change by our attitudes and behaviors than our strongest beliefs.

For example, if I held civility as a "consulter" (tentative) rather than "teller" (strong) belief, it would exercise a less consistent influence on my behavior. Suppose I got caught off guard and snapped angrily at a student. If civility were a consulter belief, I might amend my beliefs to include exceptions for students or for unusual circumstances, thus cognitively accommodating the behavior. The dissonance goes away as I change my beliefs. But if I hold civility as a teller belief, my logical response would be to maintain my conviction, apologize to the student, and work to keep myself from those unusual circumstances. In both cases, my attitudes and intentions have to deal with my beliefs, but my consulter beliefs would be influenced more easily than my teller beliefs.

Joiner beliefs. These are beliefs that influence the way we think about behavior, but are not held strongly enough to stand up to strong challenges from attitudes, intentions, and the environment. Several years ago, our school sought a government appropriation to establish a center for the study of poverty in our region. Proceeding with this required my approval. In general, I don't believe that it's particularly smart for our government to use an appropriation system, and I would rather have some private donor give us money. But my *attitude* toward the center's impact on the university and the region was very favorable; the project fit within our institutional plans (*intentions*); our congressman was a friend and sat on the House Appropriations Committee and has worked hard on behalf of his district (*experience*); and the university down the street just got appropriation money for a center on environmental law (*environment*). So my beliefs about earmarking were not intense enough to exercise their authority over my attitude, intentions, experience, and environment.

Thinking of beliefs as leaders of the other causes of behavior helps make two points. First, beliefs exercise a very strong influence over behavior and its causes. Second, beliefs vary in strength and type, as does their corresponding influence over the components of a behavioral pattern.

For us to execute enduring change in a significant pattern of behavior, we must have supportive beliefs and adequate belief strength. Or, to use the "beliefs as leader" metaphor, we need to have the right beliefs acting as tellers and sellers, supervising the other causes of behavior.

STEP FOUR: SHAPING ATTITUDES

I think the most fundamental question about our attitudes is whether we choose them or they choose us. Do attitudes descend on us, or do we have some choice in the matter? For a mood swinger like me, the answer is easy. Other people choose their attitudes, but mine just overcome me. In other words, I can't help how I feel, but you can—so shape up. Most of us carry a double standard when it comes to attitudes, expressing scorn when we encounter the bad attitudes of others while hiding behind "I can't help how I feel" when looking at ourselves.

I realize there are good people who do not enjoy a full range of choice. For some psychological or physiological reason, their emotions have been damaged and they require psychiatric attention. But, too often, those of us who are not emotionally impaired feel victimized by our attitudes. We grant them a sovereignty that renders us helpless. In one of the most supremely stupid lines ever uttered in pop music, Debby Boone wails, "It can't be wrong when it feels so right," and blah, blah, blah, "You light up my life." Not only do attitudes seem to overcome this singer emotionally, but they determine the morality of her relationship with whomever "you" is. Ms. Boone can't seem to help herself; she is surrendering to her attitude.

I remember when my nephew Tom, a very smart thirty-something guy who also happens to be one of my best friends, was dating his eventual wife, Caterina. He was trying to figure out how two people can be both honest with themselves and sensitive to each other. He observed, "I don't want her to act cheery just because she thinks I need that, not if she doesn't really feel that way."

Actually, I think maybe he does want that. It's not a bad choice for her to make if she can put her mind in charge of her disposition without feeling phony. Tom's observation makes two common assumptions about attitudes. First, attitudes just show up without being invited. We exercise little choice over how we feel. It's hard to know which side of the bed we'll wake up on. Second, it is natural and honest for us to act in accord with our feelings. To do otherwise is hypocritical.

Good leaders do not accept either of these assumptions. Frankly, nobody should. They're false. People without impaired neurological, cerebral, and psychological equipment exercise more choice over their attitudes than most of us realize.

I have a friend named Tanya who is very happily married to a wonderful guy who has to travel a lot. He and I talk pretty regularly, so I know when he's out of town. A few years ago I decided to call Tanya while her husband was gone, just to see how life was treating her. When she answered the phone, it sounded like a rock concert was going on on her kitchen counter. The screams, shouts and bursts of laughter competing with my "Tanya, is that you?" were the normal sounds of her three little rug rats going crazy. When I yelled the question, "How are you dealing with everything, Tanya?" no decibel level could have drowned out the power of her response. "I'm doing great, Bill. I don't have any choice."

As a matter of fact, Tanya was doing great because she did have a choice, and she made a healthy one. She chose to accept the steady chaos that comes with the high calling of being a parent and the principal support person for the four other people in her family. Having accepted that choice, she then chose happy and upbeat over whiny and frustrated, knowing a nasty attitude would not improve the physical circumstances of her life one iota. So Tanya *chose* to be happy. She rejected the role of victim. She chose the role of victor.

The research on attitude formation is pretty complicated. Behavioral scientists are sometimes guilty of attempting to explain and predict human behavior using formulas and tools borrowed from natural scientists. On the other hand, eager behavioral scientists like me tend to oversimplify our explanations for why people act and feel as they do. True to my own characterization, I argue that, in general, attitudes are formed and changed by associations. When I was seven years old, I went to my first major league baseball game in Chicago's Comiskey Park. It was there, worshipping my summer gods in their white wool uniforms, that I smelled my first cigar. To this day, I love that smell. It is the romantic smell of baseball on Thirty-Fifth and Shields.

Attitudes are so much the products of our associations that sometimes even what would naturally feel bad feels good to us. For example, most of the time we have a negative attitude toward pain, but by association, our attitude toward pain under certain circumstances can make it feel wonderful.

Much of what experience has taught me about attitudes has come in the athletic arena. To preserve relationships, I have been forced to choose attitudes that don't come naturally. For years, my friend Pat Cunningham and I engaged in epic tennis and racquetball battles. They would end with the two of us sprawled on the court, totally spent, while pain shot through our shoulders like a thousand needles.

At that moment of exhaustion and finality, the loser despised both of us as he recited, again, the litany of how pathetically he'd played and that surely this was the last time he would ever play this stinking sport. But for the winner, pain was the welcome messenger that reminded him of the glories of sport and the goodness of this friend heaped along side of him—this friend who on this day hated his guts.

Today my attitudes involving direct, physical competition are profoundly affected by the wars with Pat and all the other good friends with whom I've competed. The associations are so strong that when my nephew drills me in a set of tennis, the loss feels not so much like one set as like the accumulation of every set I've lost in my entire life. If I'm not careful, I will associate one event with thousands and let the feeling crush me. But I have come to realize that I don't have to relive all the losses of my life with every new loss, in tennis or anything else. If I prepare myself to respond with new associations, I loosen myself from the emotional tyranny of negative associations.

Some time ago, I was at the gym with my son, shooting baskets. After he threw down two dunks and several three-pointers while I was doing stretching exercises that would put me in a position to tie my shoes without assistance, he offered to play me in one-on-one. For his first twenty years, which were my years thirty to fifty, I owned this boy in one-on-one. Even a year or two after he had the skill to beat me, he either lacked the mental toughness or he else he realized it was better for our relationship for the less mature one of us (me) to win. But I am not a stupid man, and it was clear to me that this was his day. No matter how wily, crafty, and whiny I might be, the time had come when he would find consummate joy in destroying me. And destroy me he did.

But before he did, even before we started, I was frantically disassociating all the losses in my athletic history from the one I knew I was about to have administered. I needed to associate this imminent loss with all the wins of being Ben's dad. It worked. As I crumbled to the floor, gasping after my barrage of fouls failed to prevent the inevitable,

I crowned him the new king of one-on-one, winner-whenever-he-wanted-to-win—and it felt good.

I have discovered I can go through the same kinds of preparations that lead to the creation of positive associations with leadership patterns that are important but that I don't particularly like. For years, I dreaded doing my monthly newsletter. I would have abandoned the practice, but folks seem to really like it. At one point, I realized I needed to change my attitude toward this discipline or I'd start writing it poorly while it drove me nuts. To that end, I met with the folks who sent me information, my assistant and proofreader/editor. I told everyone what I liked least about writing this thing. What surfaced was that "writing" was the one thing I did like. The components of my dread turned out to be the organizing, searching for incomplete information, waiting for late information, patching writing time into my schedule, etc. So now, my moles and my assistant get everything ready, including a chunk of uninterrupted time. When I wake up to a "write the *Mind and Heart*" morning, I make a pot of coffee and sit down in a good mood, ready to go.

As I said above, attitude formation is very complex, and there are many points that could be made about its nature. For the purposes of this discussion on implementing new leadership behaviors and patterns, the two most important starting points are (1) rejecting the notion that we are victims of our feelings, and (2) engineering our circumstances and preparing our thinking to make positive associations with our desired behaviors.

Step Five: Organizing Intention and Environment

Although our intentions play a different role than our environment in bringing about behavioral change, I have chosen to treat these two influences together because they are both managed through planning. As stated above, intentions refer to our plans with respect to a particular behavior. Environment refers to the context in which a behavior occurs.

Often, we just expect our behavior to change in concert with changes we make in our beliefs and attitudes. If we make no changes in our lives to support what we believe and feel, the "round hole" of our habits and surroundings will reject the "square peg" of this new behavior we're after. I can recall in the late 1980s coming to grips with the impact that my romance with tradition was having on the adaptability of the institution I was leading. I had good marketing instincts, but they were bound by my skepticism of all things new. I liked classical music, classical literature, classical clothing, and classical colleges. I was not into "hip." So I vowed to become a more current leader, and I began to read books and articles on innovation. Along with my growing knowledge was an excitement I felt about getting closer to the cutting edge of things. I was putting together a new self-image. I was on my way to being contemporary. But I had neither support nor accountability to keep me on track. I simply tried to will my way into providing a different kind of leadership, and it wasn't long before the routines of my job nudged me back into the deep grooves of my old ways.

Many social psychologists have discovered that people often fail to make desired changes in their lives because they have not planned and organized for change. To use the parlance of the B-A-I-E-E-B model, people have falsely assumed that once beliefs and attitudes are headed in the same direction, behavior will automatically follow. One of the best ways I have found to calculate what I need to do with my intentions and environment is a variation on Kurt Lewin's force-field analysis. The model is pretty simple, consisting of four components, but strategies and executions are never simple. The components are:

- The desired behavior—your goal.

- An accurate assessment of your current behavior with respect to the goal.

- All the forces that propel your current behavior toward becoming your desired behavior.

- All the forces that prevent your current behavior from becoming your desired behavior.

In constructing a force-field analysis, it may be worthwhile to break down the propelling and preventing forces into beliefs, attitudes, intentions, and environmental factors. I have found, however, that the exercise is most helpful in calculating the impact of environmental influences. Hence, I have included this assessment tool in the intentions and environment discussion.

STEP SIX: STRATEGY FOR CHANGE

We can use the force-field analysis to build a three-part strategy for change:

Step 1: Weaken the forces of resistance.
Step 2: Strengthen the forces of propulsion.
Step 3: Integrate the analysis into a strategy.

In altering our leadership patterns, working on intentions and environment could be characterized as the blocking and tackling of change. It lacks glamour, frankly. Often we find our beliefs and attitudes changing on the mountaintop of a great conference or when we are lifted by witnessing a great leader. But these internal changes that occur high above life eventually collide with the street-level influences that molded the old behavior that we would like to change. Various influences contributed to the patterns we have established and will try to keep us in those patterns. Old wineskins will hold the new wine of change for a short time before they burst. It takes hard work and discipline to build a personal and organizational framework in which the inertia that binds us can be conquered.

STEP SIX: USING EXPERIENCE

From time to time, we all hear mental tapes of the lives we've lived. Some tapes make us smile, while others put beads of sweat on our brow. Some tapes are dangerous, but most are not. In fact, remembering is largely helpful, and we can use memories to support desired changes in our lives. I am quick to admit some past experiences are best dealt with professionally. Psychologists can help us find the "play" buttons for recordings suppressed or long forgotten, and sometimes they help us hit the "stop" button, or at least to change tapes. This work is important, but I believe strongly that *most* people are not shackled by *most* experiences. In other words, we have the potential to loosen the drag created by negative experiences and to create new experiences that support change.

A good way to look at the impact experience exercises over our efforts to change is from a force-field perspective. In considering a new behavioral pattern, one should ask (a) what past experiences will discourage this particular change? (b) what past experiences will encourage this change? and (c) what new experiences can be created that will encourage this change?

The benefits of this analysis lie largely in predicting the outcomes of the change we're seeking. If the change we're contemplating is largely supported by past experience (a>b), we'll have confidence when it comes time to act. If, however, there are more negative experiences associated with the new behavior we seek (a<b), then we can predict a tougher time converting beliefs, attitudes, and intentions into behavior. Also, analyzing a and b will help in the identification of new, reinforcing experiences as a part of the overall strategy for change. In virtually all areas of change, early wins are extremely important reinforcement measures.

To illustrate how past experiences influence our efforts to change, I will describe my attempt to become less timid on moral issues.

Recently the parent of a student questioned my leadership because I wasn't doing enough with respect to a situation that we agreed was bad. He wasn't aware of all I had been doing, but I think he had a point. I was not as aggressive as I should have been taking a difficult stand on this matter. I hate to admit it, but in general I am not as aggressive as I used to be. I'm afraid I release my passion most often in safe areas. One of the most stirring points of my acceptance speech as board chair of the Spokane Regional Chamber of Commerce was when I proclaimed poverty as hurtful and wrong. My conviction was inspiring. But none of the fifteen-hundred people present came up after the meeting and tried to claim that poverty was a good thing. I don't deserve any courage points for that.

One of my goals in the years ahead is to use my formal and informal power to be more aggressive in wielding moral authority. In thinking about this goal, I have found it helpful to reflect on how past experience has affected my nerve. What in my experience has reinforced my efforts to take moral stands? What has discouraged me from taking moral stands? What tapes are being played in my mind when I face something I believe is wrong?

When I analyze my past experiences, the risk-reward ratio pushes me to look at the forest rather than the trees. It's growing well. Do I really want to take on the trauma of chopping down a few morally diseased trees, especially when some of the other trees disagree sharply with what I consider to be a moral disease?

Regardless of what I hear on the old tapes, the answer to this question must be "yes" when I'm dealing with moral conflicts. I have five questions that I try always to ask whenever I feel conflict of any kind.

1. Is there a win-win resolution to this conflict?

2. If not, can I simply accommodate the position that is different from mine?

3. If not, is there a compromise will provide partial satisfaction for both sides?

4. If not, is this conflict worth resolving, or is the solution more costly than living with the problem?

5. Is this a moral issue requiring a "win-lose" resolution?

Whenever I answer "no" to the first three questions and "yes" to question five, I must act. But I must also understand that taking action on moral grounds will trigger flashbacks that can steer me in opposite directions.

Drawing on my past experiences with morally driven decisions, I have built a strategy for renewing my aggressiveness in this area. Whenever I'm faced with an opportunity to exercise moral leadership, I create a microcosm of the larger group that would be affected by my actions. The core of this representative group is the president's cabinet, but I almost always consult with people beyond those who report to me. I am pretty specific in addressing each of the preventing forces that discourage me from taking action. Having the opportunity to discuss the inevitable challenges hones and broadens my thinking while giving me a better feel for the magnitude of the reaction I can anticipate. These discussion groups have also helped reinforce my propelling experiences by identifying the benefits of past morally-based actions.

Actually, I found myself in the midst of using this strategy on a huge issue in 2000–2001. Our campus was wired with total access to the Internet on all university computers, as well as on the personal computers in all the residence-hall rooms. Regrettably, we received way too many self-reports from students that pornography was taking an evil grip on their time and thoughts. Because there have been times in which I have failed to resist pornography when it was readily accessible, I voiced many deep concerns about this issue when we were wiring our residence halls for the Internet. I ended up accepting the arguments that there are more developmentally beneficial ways to help students resist pornography than using the rather indiscriminate filters available in 1995. Several years later, we had to admit that our "developmentally beneficial" ways of discouraging misuse of the Internet did not seem to be working, for freshmen guys in particular.

I decided to study this issue and make a decision about whether to impose filters. Either changing or maintaining the status quo would be an undeniably moral action, made particularly complicated by the fact that arguments both for and against filters have the same moral foundation. At the core, the argument is loss of control versus loss of control. One group feared losing control of free inquiry, the need for self-control, and basic First Amendment rights. The other group feared losing control of their inner lives in a way that could eventually work its way into hurtful actions.

My strategy of building the microcosm and moving outward seemed to work. The groups I assembled gave me insight on the issue, courage to act, and confidence I was on the right course. In the cabinet we discussed the negative and positive experiences of the last time we took on a tough moral issue, and it was extraordinarily helpful in heading off hurtful responses. I also convened "town meetings" with students, faculty, and staff. They raised questions and made comments that I never would have considered. In the end, I decided we should subscribe to a sophisticated filtering service, and the decision was surprisingly well received.

Perhaps the most important gift presented to us by past experiences is a sharpened sense of anticipation. For us to neither listen nor learn from the past will condemn our actions to being under-informed and to the dreaded prospect of history repeating itself. We will replace studied understanding with instinctive optimism or pessimism. Clearly, we should listen to our gut instincts, but they should be given authority only after we have examined the experiences that formed them. We have no choice in *whether* we are influenced by experience. We are. Our choice is in *how* we learn from those experiences to make us more effective in our leadership.

SUMMARY

I once sat with a prospective student who'd spent his first two years of high school off on some pretty wacky social and pharmaceutical adventures. Whatever "messed up" means, he fit the bill. My young friend had taken a fast track to hell and had little hope of outgrowing his condition. His only chance for reform was an incredibly intense new belief, new attitude, new intention, and/or new environment. Because of his age and situation, salvation was initiated in the form of an extraordinarily different environment (an isolated rehabilitation school) that might work its way inward.

Beliefs, attitudes, intentions, environment, and behavior never come in equal strengths. Major changes in a person's behavioral pattern can almost always be traced to an intense change in one (initially) or more of the components that determine behavior.

The relative influence of beliefs, attitudes, intentions, environment, and experience on one's behavioral patterns will be influenced by the strength of each component. Our attempts to make significant changes in basic behavioral patterns of leadership must take into consideration different levels of intensity in the influences that lead to our actions. If we are going to take on the hard work of change, we will do well to identify whether beliefs, attitudes, intentions, or environment will do the heavy lifting for us. We can then invest our efforts in the most likely area of influence.

The question every leader must ask is whether change is worth the effort. For me, going through the process of change has been enormously gratifying. Dealing with each component has been far more enriching than onerous. Learning, renewing my spirit, reforming my plans, and restructuring my environment have all rewarded me, independent of the changes they have produced in my leadership. Beyond my renewal and enrichment, I know that students, employees, alumni, and friends of the university have a better leader than the one who was cruising on automatic pilot. Their affirmation, more than anything else, gives endurance to these new leadership patterns.

I remember seeing in Gary Trudeau's wonderful "Far Side" cartoon calendar a picture of a deeply worried-looking dog, inching forward on a tightrope. In a bubble above his anxiety-stricken expression was the caption, "I'm an old dog, and this is a new trick." At times, change feels just that way, but we can make it across the tightrope. And the benefits on the other side will make us—and those whom we lead—glad we accepted the challenge.

EPILOGUE

What's next? While I was revising this book, a Mennonite won the Tour de France and then got busted for doping up. Imagine a mild and meek Mennonite being accused of being a pill-popping racer. I heard stories of people, fish, and glaciers that got scorched by record-shattering heat. I saw a video about a father who sacrificed the normal pleasures of life so that he could be the arms and legs of his quadriplegic son who wanted to do triathlons. This father, of course, rejected heroic attributions, claiming he sacrificed nothing when he united with his son. From the different parts of the world I saw gruesome images, reminding me of our willingness to destroy each others' sons and daughters. I saw good, bad, ugly, and beautiful stuff. There are lots of changes going on. Some things stay the same.

We need leadership. We need smart leaders who recognize their frailty. We need hard-working leaders who realize that no matter how hard they work, they need help. They need help from followers who agree with them and from followers who don't. We need leadership that nurtures good followership. Warren Bennis asks, "What makes a good follower? The single most important characteristic may well be a willingness to tell the truth. In a world of growing complexity, leaders are increasingly dependent on their subordinates for good information, whether the leaders want to hear it or not" (2000, 269).

I worry about leaders who drift away from their people. I worry about leaders who equate loyalty with agreement. I just read Jonathan Aitken's book on Chuck Colson (2005). While working as President Nixon's most intimate aide, Colson's self-acknowledged fatal flaw was an iconic worship of the president. Unfortunately for himself and the country he deeply loved, Nixon viewed dissent as disloyalty. Further, he isolated himself from the Americans he led. Rather than listen to them, he distanced himself from them. He did not lead from the middle.

Who will lead us? I hope and pray it will be those Level Five leaders that have conquered the giants, "the pride and passion of man." If we can hang on for another generation or two, great leaders are on their way. Recently, I hosted university presidents and their spouses from Pepperdine, Trinity International, and Wake Forest for three days of discussion, sponsored generously by the Murdock Charitable Trust. We agreed the energy with which we face every challenge in our work lives comes from a rising generation of students carrying an unprecedented commitment to serving and reconciling humanity and the planet it occupies. Tomorrow looks great. We are training young people in the recognition that great leadership comes in serving purposes higher than ourselves.

I've enjoyed the time I've spent this summer revising this book and writing another one. It's a lot easier to write about leading than to do it. But it's more satisfying to do the work of leadership than to write about it. So, I'm headed back to the middle. Thank you for reading this book. Thank you for accepting the high call of leading. May God give you strength, and may you give your people the wisdom, energy, and confidence needed for them to join you in leadership.

References

"Spiro Agnew". 1996. In *Economist* 340, issue 7985 (September 28): 105.

Aitken, Jonathan. 2005. *Charles W. Colson: A Life Redeemed.* New York; Doubleday.

Bass, Bernard M. 1990. *Bass & Stodgill's Handbook of Leadership: Theory, Research, and Managerial Applications.* New York: The Free Press.

Bennis, Warren g. 2000. Followership. In *Managing the Dream—Reflections on Leadership and Change.* Cambridge, MA: Perseus Publishing.

--- 2001. Becoming a Leader of Leaders. In *Rethinking the Future*, by Rowan Gibson, 148-163. Naperville, IL: Nicholas Brealey Publishing.

Bennis, Warren G. and Burt Nanus. 1985. *Leaders: Strategies for Taking Charge.* New York; Harper & Row.

Bensimon, Estela and Robert Birnbaum. 1992. *How Academic Leadership Works.* San Francisco, CA: Jossey-Bass.

Blake, Robert R. and Jane S. Mouton. 1964. *The Managerial Grid.* Houston, TX; Gulf.

Burns, John. 1996. Defining Leadership: Can We See the Forest for the Trees? *The Journal of Leadership Studies* 3 no. 2: 148-157.

Burns, James McGregor. 1978. *Leadership*. New York: Harper & Row.

Cranier, Stuart. 2006. Jim Collins and Level 5 Leadership. *Management Issues* (January 3), http://www.management-issues. com/2006/5/24/mentors/jim-collins-and-level-5-leadership.asp (accessed October 7, 2009).

Cronin, Thomas E. and Genovese, Michael A. 1998. *The Paradoxes of the American Presidency*. New York, NY: Oxford University Press.

DePree, Max. 1989. *Leadership Is an Art*. New York, NY: Dell Publishing.

Fiedler, Fred E. 1967. *A Theory of Leadership Effectiveness*. New York, NY; McGraw- Hill.

Fishbein, Martin, and I. Ajzen. 1975. *Belief, Attitude, Intention, and Behavior*. Reading, MA: Addison-Wesley.

French, John and Bertram H.Raven.1959. The Bases of Social Power. In *Studies in Social Power*, ed. D. Cartwright, 150-167. Ann Arbor, MI: Institute for Social Research.

Friedman, Thomas. 2000. *The Lexus and the Olive Tree*. New York: Anchor Books.

--- 2005. *The World is Flat*. New York: Farrar, Straus and Giroux.

Goffman, Erving. 1959. *The Presentation of Self in Everyday Life*. New York: Anchor Books.

Handy, Charles. 1996. Balancing Corporate Power: A New Federalist Paper. In *Beyond Certainty*, 33-56. Boston, MA: Harvard Business Press.

Hersey, Paul and Peter Blanchard. 1969. The Life Cycle Theory of Leadership. *Training and Development Journal*, 23, no. 5: 26-34.

Hinkley, Gordon B. 2001. *Standing for Something: 10 Neglected Virtues that will Heal our Hearts and Homes*. New York: Three Rivers Press.

Janis, Irving. 1972. *Victims of Groupthink.* Boston, MA: Houghton Mifflin.

Kelly, George A. 1963. *A Theory of Personality.* New York: The Norton Library.

Kellerman, Barbara. 1999. *Cutting Edge: Leadership 2000,* ed. Barbara Kellerman and Larraine Matusak. New York: State University of New York Press.

Kouzes, James and Barry Posner. 1997. *The Leadership Challenge.* San Francisco, CA: Jossey-Bass.

Kozlowski, Steve and Mary Doherty. 1989. Integration of Climate and Leadership. *Journal of Applied Psychology* 74, no. 4 (August): 546-553.

Lee, Helen. 2003. Best Christian Places to Work: President in Sweats. *Christianity Today* (March). http://www.christianitytoday.com/ct/2003/marchweb-only/3-10-33.0.html (accessed October 10, 2009).

Lenzner, Robert and Steven S. Johnson. 1997. Seeing Things as they Really Are. *Forbes* 3, no. 2 (March 10), http://www.forbes.com/forbes/1997/0310/5905122a.html (accessed October 7, 2009).

Lewin, Kurt, Ronald Lippitt, and Ralph K. White. 1939. Patterns of Aggressive Behavior in Experimentally Created 'Social Climates'. In *Journal of Social Psychology,* 10, 271-99.

Likert, Renis. 1961. *New Patterns of Management.* New York: McGraw-Hill.

McGregor, Douglas. 1960. *The Human Side of Enterprise.* New York, NY; McGraw-Hill.

Newman, John Henry. 1852. Discourse V , section 9: Knowledge its own End. In *The Idea of a University,* 120-3. New York: Longmans, Green, and Co.

Robinson, W. P. 2009. *Incarnate Leadership: 5 Leadership Lessons from the Life of Jesus.* Grand Rapids, MI: Zondervan.

Rost, Jacob. 1991. *Leadership for the Twenty-First Century*. New York: Praeger Publishers.

Schein, Edgar H. 1992. *Organizational Culture and Leadership.*San Francisco, CA; Jossey-Bass.

Schlesinger, Arthur. 1965. *A Thousand Days.* Boston, MA: Houghton Mifflin.

Shaw, Marvin E. 1981. *Group Dynamics.* New York, NY; McGraw-Hill.

Shields, Mark. 1985. Wanted: A Gipper for the Democrats. In *The Washington Post*, December 3, A19.

Tannebaum, Robert and Warren H. Schmidt. 1958. How to Choose a Leadership Pattern. In *Harvard Business Review* 36, issue 2 (March/April): 95-101.

Tichy, Noel and Eli B. Cohen. 1997.*The Leadership Engine*. New York: Harper Collins Publishers.

Tully, Shawn. 1995. Finally, Colleges Start to Cut Their Crazy Costs. *Fortune* (May 1), http://money.cnn.com/magazines/fortune/fortune_archive/1995/05/01/202479/index.ht (accessed October 9, 2009).

Warren, Rick. 2002. *The Purpose Driven Life*. Grand Rapids, MI: Zondervan.

Yukl, Gary. 2005. *Leadership in Organizations*. Upper Saddle River, NJ: Pearson-Prentice Hall.

Recommended Resources
not Cited in the Text

Bass, B. M. 1994. *Improving Organizational Effectiveness through Transformational Leadership.* Thousand Oaks, CA: Sage Publications.

Collins, J. 2001. *Good to Great.* New York, NY: Harper & Collins.

Drucker, P. F. 1993. *Managing for the Future: The 1990s and Beyond.* New York, NY: Penguin Books.

Gardner, J. W. 1990. *On Leadership.* New York: The Free Press.

Greenleaf, R. K. 1977. Servant *Leadership: A Journey into the Nature of Legitimate Power and Greatness.* Mahwah, NJ: Paulist Press.

Heifitz, R. A., & Linsky, M. 2002. "Leadership on the Line: Staying Alive through the Dangers of Leading." *Harvard Business School Press.*

Hill, L. A. 2008. Where Will We Find Tomorrow's Leaders? *Harvard Business Review* (January).

Jaworski, J. 1996. *Synchronicity: The Inner Path of Leadership.* San Francisco, CA: Berrett-Koehler Publishers.

Kotter, John P. 1996. *Leading Change.* Boston, MA: Harvard Business School Press.

Nouwen, H. 1989. *In the Name of Jesus: Reflections on Christian Leadership*. New York, NY: Crossroad Publishing.

Robbins, S. P., and T.A. Judge. 2007. *Organizational Behavior*, 12th Edition. Boston, MA: Prentice Hall.

Spears, L. C. 1995. *Reflections on Leadership*. New York: John Wiley & Sons, Inc.

Tichy, N. M. & Bennis, W. G. 2007. *Judgment, How Winning Leaders Make Great Calls*. Penguin Group.

Wheatley, M. J. 1994. *Leadership and the New Science*. San Francisco, CA: Berrett-Koehler Publishers.

Made in the USA
Lexington, KY
20 October 2011